How Do I Get Started With SketchUp Free

R D TURNER

PARTRIDGE

To order additional copies of this book, contact
Toll Free 800 101 2657 (Singapore)
Toll Free 1 800 81 7340 (Malaysia)
orders.singapore@partridgepublishing.com

www.partridgepublishing.com/singapore

PART 1
-
HOW DO I GET STARTED WITH SKETCHUP FREE
-
THE BASICS

To my wife Nida and my sisters Julia,

Maureen and Elaine.

You are the ground on which my life has been built

Acknowledgments

The author would like to thank the contributors to the 3D Warehouse who have made available for download the varying pieces of model furniture shown in the projects. The author would also like to thank the students of the Computer Aided Design Section of Pusat Pembangunan Belia (Youth Development Centre) for their unsuspecting contribution during the books development.

General Contents of Part One

For Detailed Contents See page 333

Introduction

This book is designed as a self-learning aid on how to use SketchUp Free the web-based program. The book covers the basics and more advanced methods on how to use SketchUp Free. It has been written to assist students at School, College and University who are beginning a course of study that incorporates in their syllabus, 3D Modelling using SketchUp. The book will also be of benefit for anyone who just wants to learn SketchUp. The book has been written around the web-based free version of SketchUp, but that does not mean it cannot be used with earlier or later versions of SketchUp. The instructions given in the book, with slight adjustments depending on the SketchUp version being used, will still let you learn how to produce 3D Models.

The book will be of assistance to teachers in the teaching of 3D Modelling using SketchUp. It can be used as a stand-alone introduction to provide full basic coverage in getting started with SketchUp Free or other versions of SketchUp.

Part One introduces the basic tools and techniques to produce both mechanical and very simple architectural models. The amount of time spent in learning on Part One should not exceed 60 hours and in fact, you should be up and running in as little as 3hours. Part Two introduces more advanced modelling methods and tech-niques. The amount of time spent in learning Part Two should not exceed 90 hours. The hours given will give teachers setting up a course of study some guidance as to the maximum length of time that should be given.

The book is very popular with students because it does not contain masses of information, only the basic requirements. This has allowed them to work effectively on their own and at their own pace. The book uses easy to follow instructional learning blocks that introduce a new piece or pieces of information about how to use the Tools and Techniques in producing 3D Models, so gradually building up the student's knowledge and skills.

The teaching method is very much a *take you by the hand* approach, which is what is wanted until the student gains confidence.

Though the book has been designed for self-learning, it has not been designed to replace the teacher. The advantage to the teacher, when using the book, is that it frees them from the 'Whiteboard' and so can spend more time on demonstrations, detailed explanations and most importantly with the individual student. It is also anticipated that the teacher will supply additional drawing exercises to add to those given in the book.

Starting Out

As a *Beginner*, you are just about to start on what really will be a "Voyage of Discovery", but you are in good hands as the book has been purposely written for Beginners. If I can give you any advice before you start it is this; be very patient, you are about to discover the uses of many tools and techniques of SketchUp Free or whatever version of SketchUp being used, and this takes time. Also, remember as you are reading the book; describing how to use the commands takes far longer than actually carrying them out. If you bear these two points in mind I am sure that your "Voyage of Discovery" will be an enjoyable one.

HEALTH and SAFETY

WARNING

USING YOUR COMPUTER CAN BE DANGEROUS

**IF YOU CAN ANSWER <u>ALL</u> OF THE FOLLOWING QUESTIONS THEN YOU ARE OK TO PROCEED TO
PAGE ONE
BUT
IF YOU CANNOT ANSWER <u>ALL</u> OF THE QUESTIONS THEN YOU NEED TO STUDY THE INFORMATION SHOWN ON THE NEXT FEW PAGES.**

QUESTIONS

QU.1 – What produces an **RSI**.

QU.2 – State at least TWO common health issues associated with the use of a computer.

QU.3 – Give **Three** examples of how you can prevent Eyestrain.

QU.4 – When using a computer give **TWO** Precautions which can reduce the risk of accidents when dealing with **computer cables.**

QU.5 – When using the computer what Safeguards can be taken to minimize the risk of accidents.

Health & Safety

Health

There are hundreds if not thousands of books that have been written about Health and Safety, this book though is not one of them. But as computer users, we should be aware of the problems that are associated with their use. Regular use of the computer can lead to different health issues such as back, neck, hand and eye problems. All of which can be avoided if we take the necessary precautions.

RSI – A **Repetitive Strain Injury** or Injuries occur when you repeat over and over again for long periods the same movement causing damage to parts of the body, mainly arm, wrist, fingers, shoulders, neck and back.

The main causes of RSI to arms, wrist and fingers –
a) Using the mouse for long periods.
b) Typing for extended periods.
c) Typing on a poorly designed keyboard.
d) Incorrect seating so that arms become stressed because they are in an unfamiliar position.
e) The computer table (workbench) is at the incorrect height to suit the person using it producing the same result as (d) above.

The main causes of RSI to the shoulder, neck and back –
a) Non-adjustable chair.
b) Adjustable chair set to the wrong height.
c) A computer table is at the incorrect height to suit the person using it.
d) A fixed positioned monitor or computer screen.
e) An adjustable monitor or computer screen set at the wrong angle for the person that is using it.

To avoid the majority of problems with RSI just make sure that –
a) **You use an adjustable chair set to the correct height for you.**
b) Ideally, the correct height should allow you to –

- Look down within your normal range of vision at the monitor or computer screen.
- Be in a position whereby your arms are in a comfortable position for typing or using the
mouse.
- Have your back and shoulders supported.
- Have your feet rest comfortably on the floor or
footrest.
- Sit comfortably with your knees bent at 90° so that
Your legs are not under any stress.

c) Your monitor or computer screen can be tilted to a comfortable viewing angle and the height can be adjusted to avoid putting any stress on your neck and shoulders.
d) Ideally making sure that your computer table is suitable for you **before you buy it.**
e) And probably the most important of all prevention methods, and the cheapest – Take a break for 5-10 minutes every 60-90 minutes by standing up and having a walk around the room.

Another health problem when using the computer and looking at the monitor or the computer screen for long periods is eyestrain. If you are rubbing your eyes as though they are itching or if you have got something in your eyes, it is a good indication that you are straining your eyes. Another indication is if you start to get double vision or objects on the screen start to become blurred. Eyestrain can also bring on headaches which of course can make you feel real miserable. So how to avoid eyestrain –

a) Have a rest – Take a 5/10 minute break every hour or an hour and a half.

b) Prevent the sun from shining onto the screen by having blinds or curtains on the windows

c) When using lights use lights that disperse the light evenly.

d) When using lights make sure the light does not shine directly onto the screen.

e) Sit comfortably keeping your head at least 500mm (20inches) from the screen.

f) Do not stare at the screen for long periods, look away at regular intervals.

g) If you have been prescribed glasses **wear them.**

h) If you are still having eye problems after taking the precautions mentioned then go and have an eye test.

Safety

Most if not all accidents when dealing with computers can be avoided if simple precautions are applied. To help reduce the risk of an accident when you are working on your computer at home or work just make sure of the following –

a) When dealing with the various cables –

• Make sure that they are not placed where people could trip or stand on.

• To avoid the above just make sure the cables are secured safely.

• Avoid overloading power points – just **one** plug to each socket.

b) Food and drink should not be placed near a computer

c) Food and drink should not be placed near computer equipment such as –

• The Keyboard, Printer, Scanner, Monitor.

d) You should have adequate space around the desk so people can move freely.

e) To avoid people tripping over items the items should be stored out of the way.

f) When selecting a computer table (workbench) make sure it is strong enough to support the computer and equip- ment.

g) To work comfortably make sure the Heating/Air condition- ing and ventilation is suitable for the working environment.

The answers to all the questions are in the information given on health and safety. In not giving direct answers to the questions I hope by reading through the information to find the answers, has made you more aware when using your computer of health and safety matters.

So

Be Healthy be Safe

And

Now Go

And Learn How

To Use

SketchUp Free

PART ONE

-

THE BASICS

The Basics - Part One

BEFORE YOU START

To learn the very basics of SketchUp Free only takes a few hours of practice. The program is **designed to get you "up and running" in the shortest of time.** If you follow these **guidelines;**

1. **Be focused on what you are doing.**
2. **Follow step by step the instruction given in this book.**
3. **Practice what you have been shown, (Very Important).**
you will very quickly master the basics of SketchUp.

To start SketchUp Free it would be **advisable** to have one of the **following browsers** installed on your computer -

The browser I use for SketchUp Free is Chrome.
Several ways can be used to start SketchUp Free but the one I recommend when accessing SketchUp Free for the first time is by typing -
sketchup.com/products/sketchup-free into your browser search box.

To open SketchUp Free

- In the browser search box; type -
  sketchup.com/products/sketchup-free
- Then pick the search button.
- From the web sites shown you are looking for - **SketchUp Free.**

The Basics - Part One

SketchUp Websites

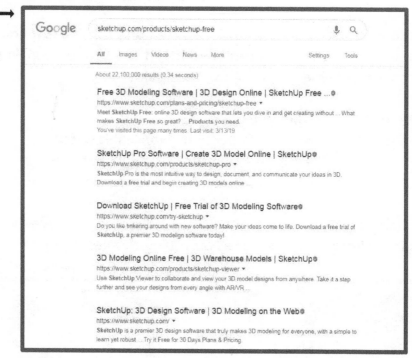

- **The web sites shown on your screen might be different to the one above but just open the one that shows - SketchUp Free**

This takes you to the opening SketchUp window

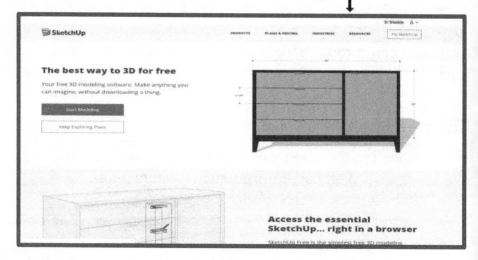

The Basics - Part One

To get some information about SketchUp Free scroll down.

To open SketchUp Free -

- Pick the - **Start Modeling** Button.
- This takes you to the **Trimble Sign-in page.**

- On Completing the Sign-in details You will be shown the SketchUp Free opening window, a **pulsating SketchUp Logo** ⌐

Once it stops
Pulsating -

- In the Privacy notice, pick the OK button to agree with the cookie policy and the Terms of service.
- On picking the OK button you get displayed a Welcome to SketchUp Window ⌐

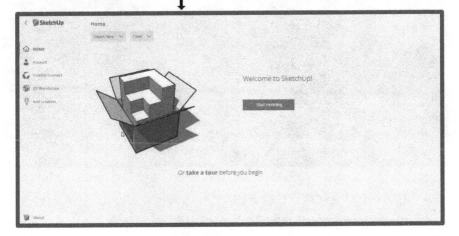

The Basics - Part One

- Pick - **take a tour**.
- In the graphic Screen displayed select the **Start Tour option.**

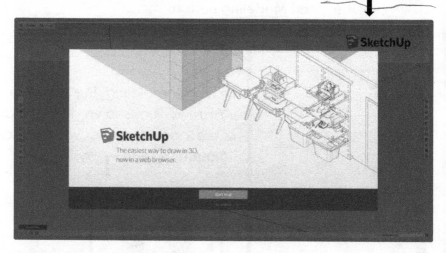

- This will show you the General layout of the SketchUp Free graphics screen and information on the icons displayed in the Home Bar.

General Layout of the Graphic Screen

- Clicking the **OK...Got it** button - will show you information on other icons displayed in SketchUp Free.

The Basics - Part One

Other Icons

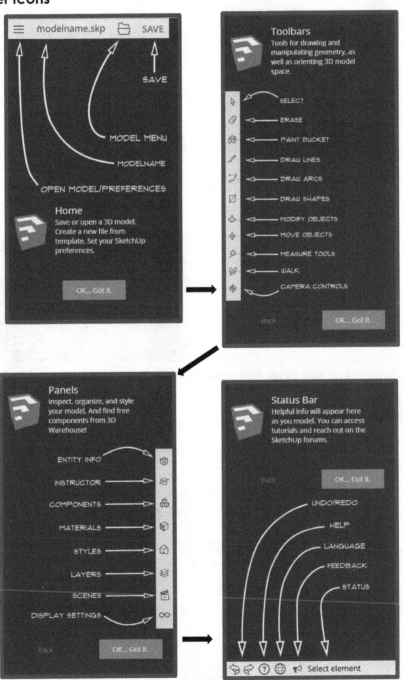

The Basics - Part One

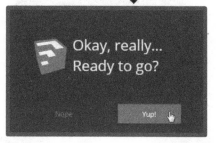

- Pick the **Great...Let's go!** Button
- Pick the **Yup!** button in the enquiry window.

You now have the **opening screen view** -

Opening Screen View

The Basics - Part One

The Toolbar on the left of the screen, which comes under the heading Toolbars (see page 5), can be grouped into the following panels -

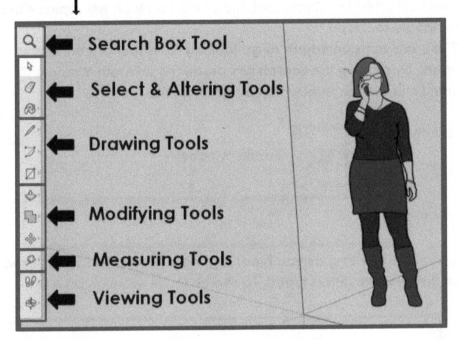

In the varying groups, **if the icon has an arrowhead beside it, it indicates that there are other tools associated with that icon,** for example; **Selecting the Rectangle tool icon reveals five other drawing tools -**

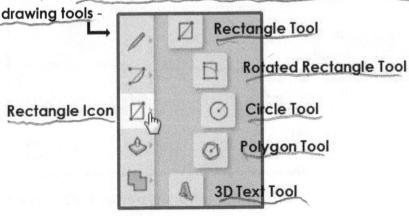

A point to remember when selecting an icon from the revealed group of icons, is - on completion of the work with the selected tool, that tools icon becomes the default in the main tool toolbar. If you selected the Circle tool, the circle tool icon will replace the rectangle tool icon.

If you are not sure where to go looking for a tool or contents of a panel, by picking the Search Box produces a Results Window. You then Enter the name of what you want to find.

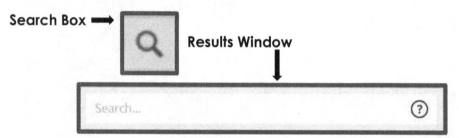

Search Box ➡

Results Window

You will notice that **as you type, suggestions are displayed based on the opening letters typed. To search for information on Axes -**

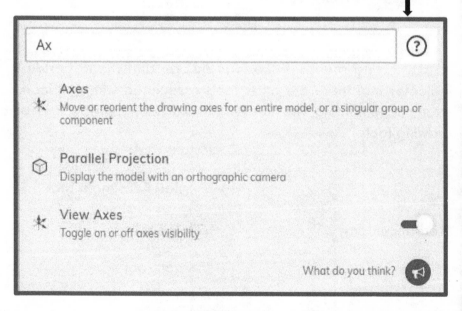

As you type, suggestions on the letters typed are displayed.

The Panel Bar on the right of the screen (page 4/5), contains the varying panels that allow you to create; layer names, alter settings, apply information. You will be using this toolbar quite often throughout your SketchUp training. **I will go into more detail as and when you need to use the varying panels.**

- **Have a go at picking some of the toolbar options to see what they contain.**
- When you have finished practising – **Close SketchUp by picking the Close icon in the top Right corner.**
- You get an enquiry message

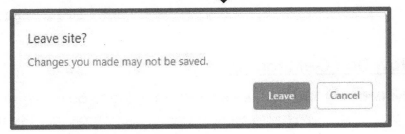

- Pick the **Leave** button

How Do I Start SketchUp Free

- In the browser search box; type - **SketchUp Free**

- Pick the search button.

- Pick **SketchUp Free** from the web sites shown

- In the opening SketchUp window pick **Start Modeling**

- You get the **pulsating SketchUp Logo then the Welcome to SketchUp window - Pick - Start Modelling.**

- **This produces** the **SketchUp Free graphic screen.**

How Do I Get Started

The first thing is to set the units we are going to be using. SketchUp Free has as its default unit feet and inches (imperial). **The unit we want are millimetres - Metric units. Two methods can be used** to set the units - **through the Panel Bar** or from **a millimetre Template File.**

Using the Template File

- In the **Home Bar** - top left in the graphics screen - pick the **Open Model/ Preferences icon**

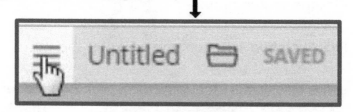

- This takes you the **Welcome Window.**
- **Pick the Create New Box.**

- From the options displayed **select the - Simple Template Millimeters**

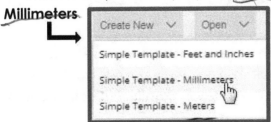

- **You are returned to the graphics screen with the modelling environment set to millimetres. (To complete the setup** you use the **Model Info Panel** - see the **Second Method to see how to carry out these settings).**

The **Second Method** that can be used to set the unit to millimetres is by -

- Picking the **Model Info** panel icon towards the very bottom of the **Panel Bar** on the **Right** of the **Graphics Screen.**

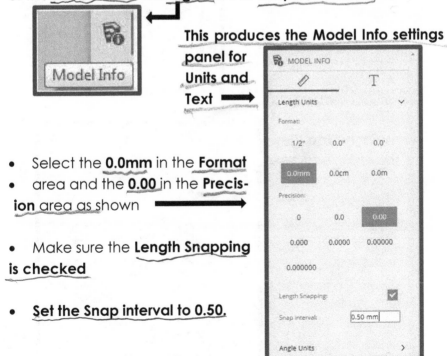

This produces the Model Info settings panel for Units and Text ➡

- Select the **0.0mm** in the **Format** area and the **0.00** in the **Precision** area as shown ➡

- Make sure the **Length Snapping** is checked

- **Set the Snap interval to 0.50.**

- Close the **Model Info** Settings page -

MODEL INFO   X

The next change is in the viewpoint that we are going to start modeling in. The default is **Perspective and Front- Right ISO** (Isometric). We will start our models in **Parallel Projection and a Top View.**

- Pick the **Views** Panel icon from the **Panel Bar.**
- This opens the **Views** panel page.

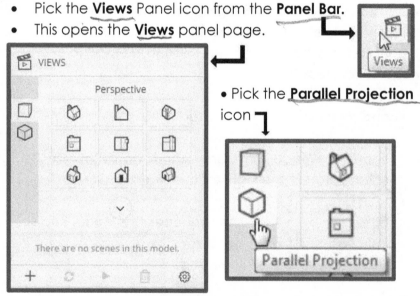

- Pick the **Parallel Projection** icon

- Then the **Top View** as shown

- Close the **Views** page -

- This produces the Screen View as shown ⌐

How Do I Create Shapes

- To choose a shape click the shape wanted from the Draw Tools on the left of the screen.
- Pick the **Rectangle Tool icon**.

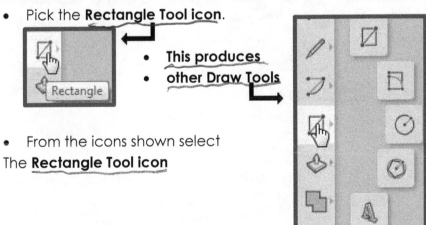

- This produces
- other Draw Tools

- From the icons shown select

The **Rectangle Tool icon**

The Basics - Part One

- Position the pencil at the **origin point** of the axes and click.

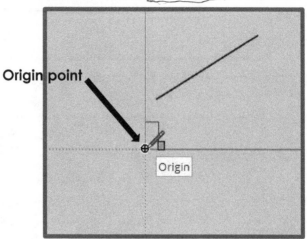

- **Move the cursor diagonally down and to the right.**
- In the **Dimension edit box** in the bottom right-hand corner enter the **Size 2000,1000**

- Press the **Enter Key.**

The **Drawing Area** Looks Like This.

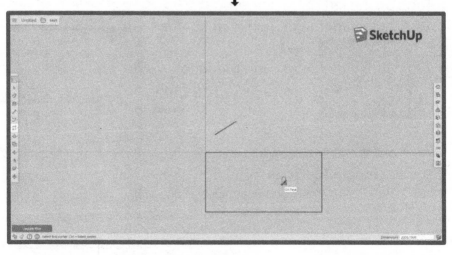

To Change to an ISOMETRIC Viewpoint.

- **Go to -**
- The **Views Panel.**
- Click **Front-Right Iso view** from the options displayed.

- **Close the Views Panel.**
- The Drawing Area View is as shown.

Drawing Area View

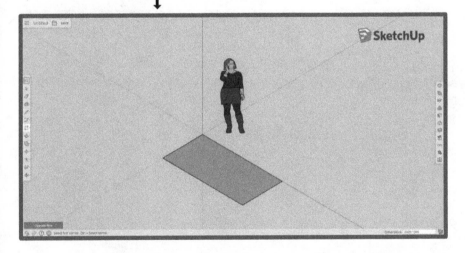

How Do I Create 3D Objects

- From the **Tools Toolbar,** select the **Push/Pull icon**

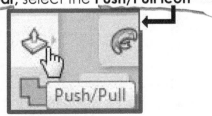

The group of tools displayed can be ignored as the Tool required (Push/Pull) has been selected.

- Position the **Push/Pull icon** in the **centre** of the rectangle – click.
- **Drag the Push/Pull icon up.**
- At the **Distance edit box**, enter **1500** – the height of the block.
- Press the Enter key.

This produces a Drawing Area View as shown .

Drawing Area View After Using the Push/Pull Tool

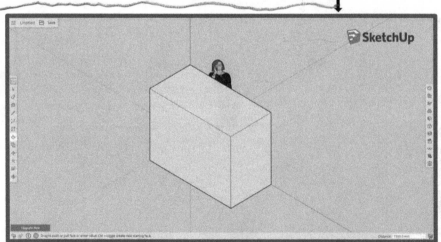

You now need to practice what has been shown so far.

- **Close SketchUp.**
- **You get an enquiry message**

Leave site?

Changes you made may not be saved.

Leave   Cancel

- Pick the **Leave** button.

As a beginner, when starting SketchUp Free, get into the habit of setting the environment shown. Don't be tempted to start modelling in the opening 3D (Isometric) view. When producing 3D Models of buildings or mechanical parts, you will find, initially, that the model is easier to produce if you start laying out the model in a 2D setting. Once you have the general layout/shape of the model then change to a 3D environment.

The next few exercises we will see how to produce **shapes in 2D** and the **model in 3D.**

To produce a Block **2000 x 1000 x 2000.**

Use the second method shown to set the unit.

- **Start SketchUp Free.**

- Set the Unit to - **Millimeters** - precision **2 decimal places (0.00).**
    o Make sure the **Length Snapping is checked**
    o **Set the Snap interval to 0.50.**

- Change the View to **Parallel** and the viewpoint to **Top View.**
- **This produces a 2D viewpoint.**

- Using the **Rectangle Tool** draw a rectangle having a Length of **2000mm** and a width of **1000mm.**
- Change the viewpoint to a **Front-Right Iso view.**

- Using the **Push/Pull** tool produce a block from the Rectangle having a height of **2000mm.**

- The completed block will be the same as that shown in the **Drawing Area View.**

The Drawing Area View of the 2000 x 1000 x 2000mm Block.

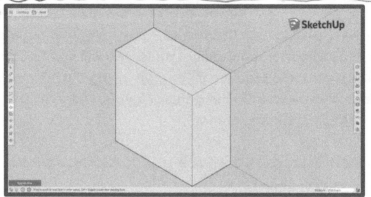

Exercise

- Produce a **3D model of a circle positioned at the bottom left corner of the rectangle** having a **diameter of 1000mm and a height of 2000mm.**
- Produce a **3D model of a 6 sided polygon positioned to the right of the rectangle** and with **one side parallel to the Red Axis.** The **radius of the polygon is 500mm and the height 2000mm.**
- Remember to go back to a **Top view before you start the exercise.**
- On completion, your models will be the same as that shown in the **Drawing Area View.**

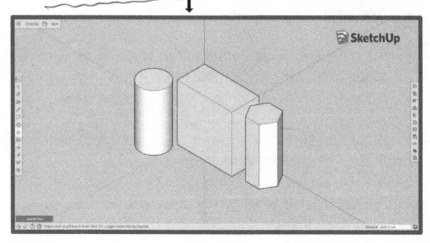

Zoom, Pan, Orbit

You will find that at some time during the models' development you will need to change the view on the screen. The three most common options to change the view is through the use of the Zoom, Pan and Orbit tools.

Zoom

This tool allows you to get in close to where you are working or move back far enough to view the whole of the model.

- From the **View Tools** on the left of the graphics screen, select the **Orbit icon.** From the **group displayed** pick the icon **Zoom**

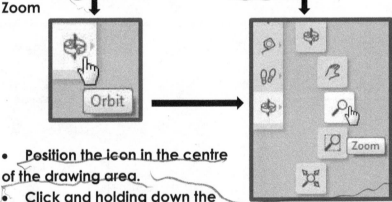

- Position the icon in the centre of the drawing area.
- Click and holding down the pick button on the mouse move UP or diagonally towards the top right or left corner of the drawing area. The objects appear larger because you have Zoomed In.
- Still holding down the pick button on the mouse move DOWN or diagonally towards the bottom left or right corner of the drawing area. The objects appear smaller because you have Zoomed Out.
- Pick the **Select Arrow from the Tools Toolbar**

Zoom - Window

This tool allows you to zoom in on specific parts of your model. From our model, let's say the cylinder.

The Basics - Part One

- From the **View Tools** Select the **Zoom icon.**
- From the **group displayed** pick the icon **Zoom Window**

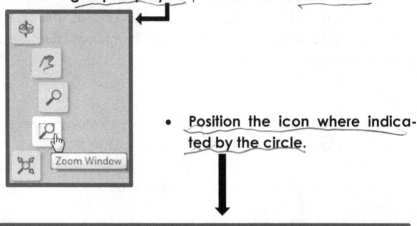

Zoom Window

- **Position the icon where indicated by the circle.**

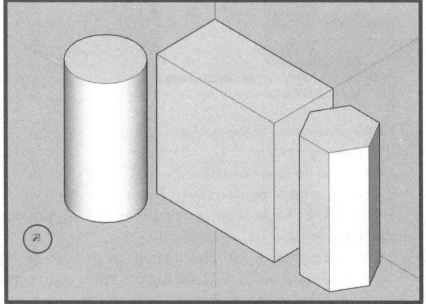

- **Pick and holding down the pick button** on the mouse **move diagonally towards the top right of the cylinder.** As you move a **window frame appears.**

- **Position the window frame so it completely surrounds the** cylinder - about where Indicated.

Page 20

Position the Window Frame Where Indicated By the Circle ⌐

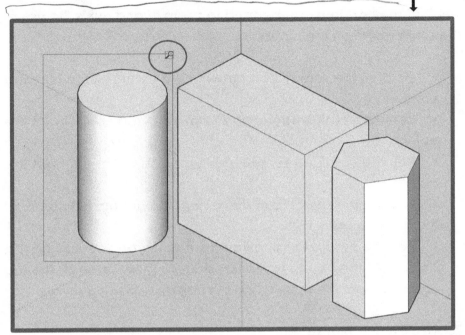

- **Release the pick button.**

- **This produces a view as shown.** ⌐

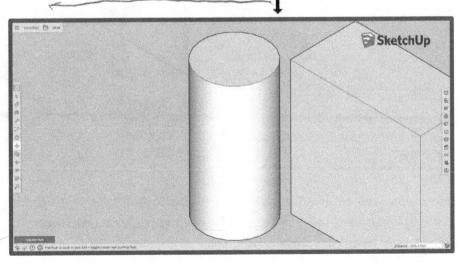

Zoom Using the Mouse

Another method that can be used to zoom in and out is the use of the scroll wheel on the mouse.

- Position the select icon arrow in the centre of the drawing area.
- Roll the scroll wheel away from you–you zoom in on the object.
- Roll the scroll wheel towards you–you zoom out from the object.
- Position the select icon arrow near the bottom left corner of the drawing area.
- Roll the scroll wheel away from you–you zoom in on the object but the object (cylinder) starts to move towards the top right corner of the screen and out from the drawing area.

Zoom Using the Mouse

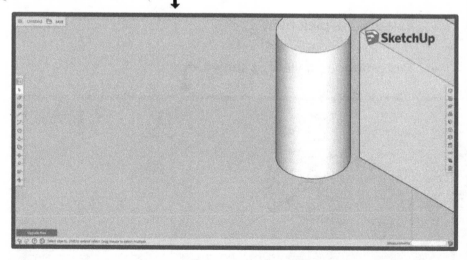

Leave the select icon arrow at the bottom left corner of the drawing area and roll the scroll wheel towards you until the three objects are visible as shown.

Scroll until the Three Objects are as shown

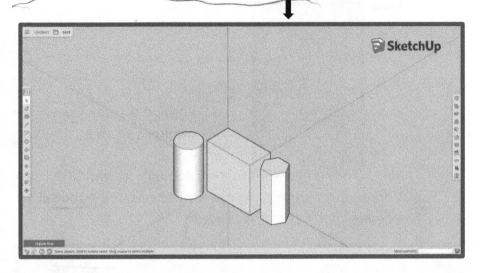

(You might have to re-position the arrow and scroll to get the objects in position, but you get the idea).

Remember, when scrolling with the mouse try and position the select icon arrow in the centre of the screen to keep the objects working on in view.

Pan

When you zoom in on an object other parts of the drawing are not visible on the screen. When you need to work on these none visible parts the PAN tool lets you drag them back into view without having to zoom out.

- From the **View Tools** on the left of the graphics screen, select the

  Zoom Window icon.

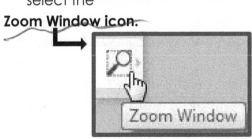

- From the **group displayed** pick the icon - **Pan**

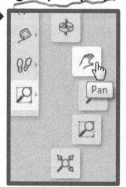

- Position the **Pan icon** in the **centre** of the drawing area.
- **Holding down** the pick button on the mouse drag the pan icon until the **model** is in the **centre** of the drawing area.

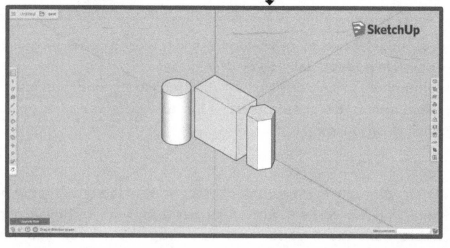

- Remember, the Pan Tool lets you move the model in any direction without having to zoom out to another viewpoint.

Orbit

The Orbit tool lets you change your viewpoint to any point around the object.

- Press the **Right** button on the mouse and select **Exit**.
- From the **View Tools** on **the left of the graphics screen,** select the **Pan icon**.

Pan Icon

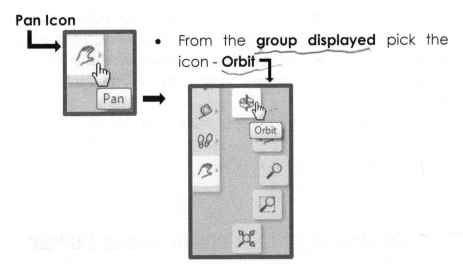

- From the **group displayed** pick the icon - **Orbit**

- **Position the orbit tool in the centre of the drawing area.**
- **Holding down the pick button on the mouse drag the orbit icon up** – notice how your viewpoint changes.
- **Still holding down the pick button drag the icon to the right** – this gives you the front view of the models.
- **Drag to the left** – your model rotates to give you a viewpoint looking at the ends of the model.

Orbit Tool View

Remember, the Orbit tool lets you view your model from any direction. If you hold the Shift Key down whilst using the Orbit tool it will produce the Pan tool so you can pan to a different position. On releasing the Shift key you are returned to the Orbit Tool.
Try it out,

- **Practice** using the different **View Tools.**
- **On Completion.**
- **Close** SketchUp Free.
- Enquiry Box – **Leave.**

How Do I Use Other Tools and Modelling Techniques

- **Start SketchUp Free**
- Use the **Simple Template** – Millimeters from the **Create** New in the Welcome Window - This takes you to the Graphic Screen.
- Set the Unit to - **Millimeters** - precision **2 decimal places (0.00).**
  - o Make sure the Length Snapping is checked
  - o Set the Snap interval to 0.50
- **Produce a Parallel Projection View and a Top View.**

Line Tool
The Line Tool is used mainly for creating shapes.
To produce a square shape measuring 1000mm x1000mm x 1000mm;

- Click on the **Line Tool** icon in the **Tools Toolbar** -

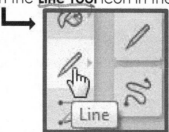

The group of tools displayed can be ignored as the tool required (Line) has been selected.

- Position the **Line tool** at the **Origin point** and Click.

- Move the **Line tool** to the **Right along the Red axis line** and in the length edit box, enter **1000.**

- Move the Line tool **vertically down** and again enter **1000.**

- Move the Line tool **to the left** – notice how the line **automatically aligns with the Red Axis and locks in position when on the Green Axis to produce the horizontal line** – click.

- **Move up and back to the origin** – click.

- This produces a closed square as shown in the **Drawing Area View.**

Drawing Area View

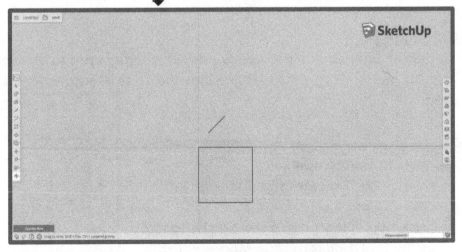

- Change your viewpoint too - **Front-Right Iso.**

- Using the **Push/Pull tool** produce a **vertical height of 1000mm** as shown.

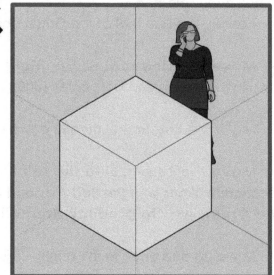

- This has produced a 3D model of a cube block measuring 1000 x 1000 x 1000.

You can now put a square hole 500mm x 500mm through the left face and a circular hole of a diameter of 500mm through the right face. To position the holes accurately you can use Guidance lines.

Guidance Lines

Guidelines are used to accurately position shapes used to create your 3D model. To produce Guidelines the Tape Measure Tool is used.

To Draw the Square Hole.
- Pick the **Tape Measure Tool** icon in the Tools Toolbar -

The group of tools displayed can be ignored as The Tool required (Tape Measure) has been selected.

- **Position the tape icon at mid-point on the left vertical edge of the left face – the point turns a light blue colour.**

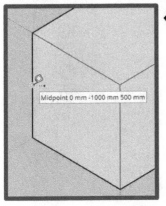

○ **Click to locate the point. Drag the icon to the right – a red line is shown indicating you are parallel with the red axis.**

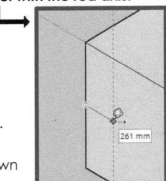

- Type **250** and press the Enter Key.

- A **dotted vertical guideline** is shown 250mm from the selected edge.

A Guideline is produced 250mm from the edge.

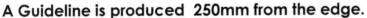

Guideline ■——▶

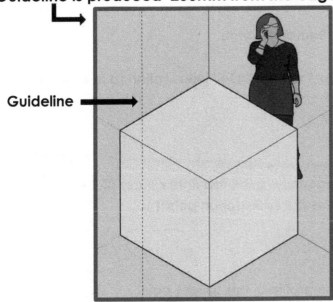

- Repeat the process for the remaining 3 guidelines.
- This produces

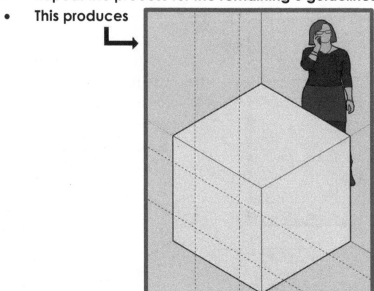

The guidelines have produced the profile of the square hole.

- **Zoom in** on the square profile.

- Pick the **Rectangle tool.**

- **Position at the bottom left intersection (a red x indicates the intersection point)**

- Click.

- **Drag diagonally to the top right corner of the guidelines (a red x indicates the intersection point)**

- Click.

This produces the profile of the square hole.

Square Hole Profile

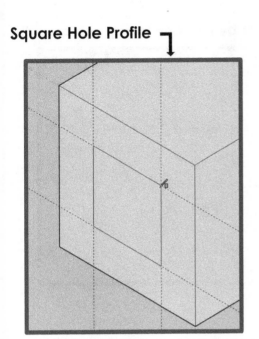

- **Zoom** by using the **scroll wheel** on the mouse, until you can see all of the block.
- Select the **Push/Pull tool** and position in the centre of the **square profile just created.**

- **The selected area becomes a series of dots as shown –**

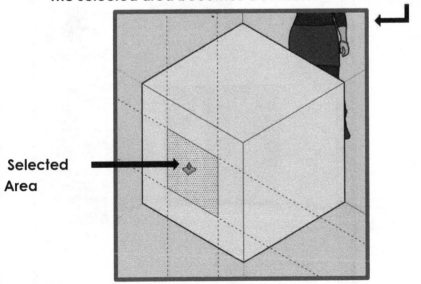

Selected
Area

- **Click the pick button and move diagonally right until the Push/Pull icon is on the edge of the block.**

- A red square will appear by the icon to say you are - On Edge.

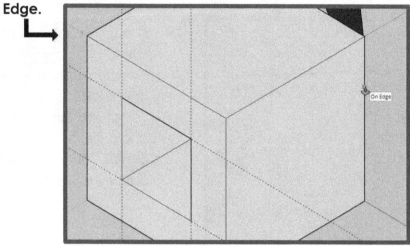

- Click.
- Orbit to see the result.

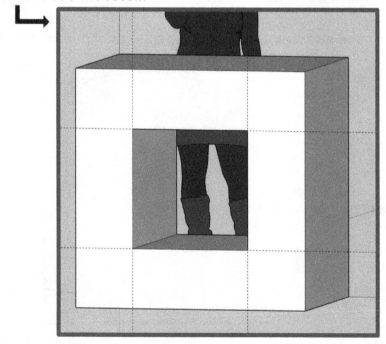

As can be seen, a hole has been produced in the block. The Push/Pull tool will create holes, hollows and extrusions.

Erase Tool

The Erase tool is used to remove unwanted parts of the model. To see how to use the Erase tool you can remove the guidelines used for producing the square hole.

- Select the **Erase Tool** icon from **Tools Toolbars**

(Notice No hidden group of tools as there was no arrowhead by the side of the Erase icon.

- **Position the circle attached to the icon over the top horizontal guideline.**
- **The corner of the erase icon is touching the line.**

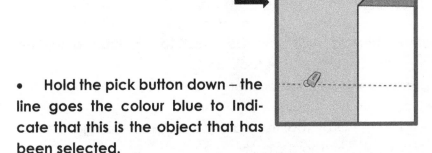

- **Hold the pick button down – the line goes the colour blue to indicate that this is the object that has been selected.**
- **Now release the pick button and the guideline is erased.**
- **You could also use this technique –**
- **Drag the erase tool close to the guideline to be erased,**

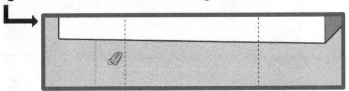

- Hold the **pick button down** and then **drag onto the object,** when the selected object turns to the **colour blue release** the pick button. This method can be used to select a number of objects.

- Try out the two methods on the remaining three guidelines.

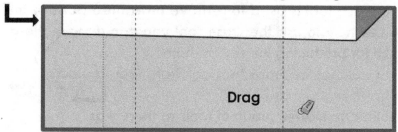

If you erase an object by mistake –

- Select the **Undo icon** in **the bottom left corner of the graphics screen**

The Erase tool can be used for other functions, these will be shown later in the course.

Another method that can be used **to produce guidelines** is through the use of the **Line tool.**

To produce the 500mm diameter Hole Through the Right Face of the Block.

- Use the **Orbit tool** to rotate the block so the right side of the block is shown more clearly.

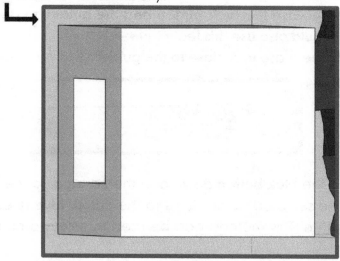

- Use the **Line tool** to produce guidelines to find the centre of the right face
- **Select the Line Tool icon.**

Remember - whatever tool is visible in the tools toolbar becomes the default tool. Providing that is the tool you want to use there is no need to re-select it from the group of tools displayed.

- **Move on to the top edge of the right face until a blue dot appears indicating you are on the midpoint of the edge.**
- **Click.**
- **Move** the icon vertically **down to the midpoint of the bottom edge** of the right face.
- **Click.**
- **Move the icon on to the midpoint of the right edge.**
- **Click.**
- **Move the icon horizontally left to the midpoint of the left edge.**
- **Click.**

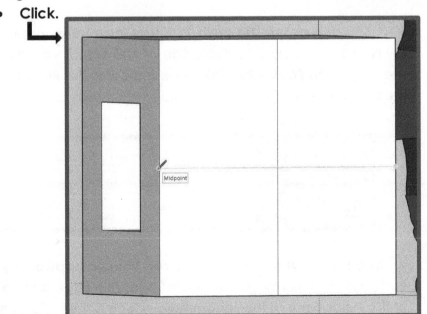

- Then use the **Circle tool.**
- **Position** the circle tool **at the intersection of the guidelines**
- Click
- **Drag outwards and enter 250 at the Radius edit box.**
- **Select the Push/Pull tool.**
- **Position in one of the quadrants (arcs) of the circle,** notice **Only** that quadrant contains the dots, so **only that quadrant would be worked on.**
- Move the Push/Pull tool outside the quadrant and that area gets selected.

Remember the Line tool is used mainly to produce profiles

- **Having drawn the circle - Erase the Guidelines**
- **Select the Push/Pull tool** to produce the hole.

To produce the hole, you need to indicate when the Push/Pull tool is either on the inner face or on the edge of the inner face of the square hole.

- Click and **move the Push/Pull tool icon horizontally left.**
- When you come to the edge of the block you get the message - **On Edge** – but **this edge indicates the Right face of the block** which is the face the circle was drawn on.

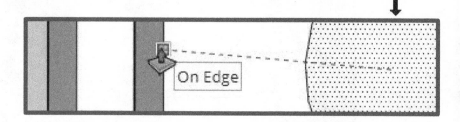

- **Keep moving the icon until a red square appears by the Push/Pull icon to say you are - On Edge. This edge is the edge of the inside face of the square hole, which is the face wanted.**

On The Inside Edge of the Block

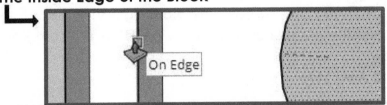

- Click.
- **The hole appears in the Right face of the block.**
- **Orbit the block** so you can see clearly the hole produced.

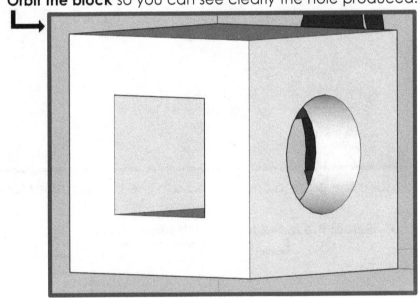

How Do I Group Objects

A Group is a combination of entities that make up an object into one unique part. For example a table top or a chair seat. Groups are extremely useful as they prevent lines that are drawn on a group from merging, preventing distortion when modifying tools are used in the construction of joining parts. Groups allow parts to be copied and moved easily.

To create groups you use the "Make Group" tool after selecting what you want in the group.

To illustrate how important groups are -
- Change your viewpoint to a **Front Right-View Iso.**
- **Scroll** so your Drawing Area View looks the same as that shown -

Drawing Area View ⌐

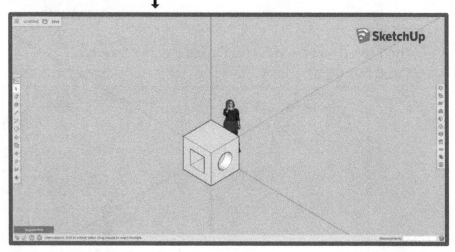

To Move the cube along the red axis line by using the Move Tool

- **Select the Move tool from the Tools Toolbar**

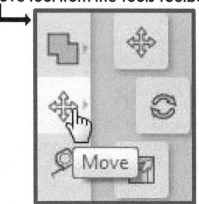

- Position the tool on the **Right Vertical edge** of the block as shown. The selected line turns to the **colour blue** and the message - **On Edge** – appears.

The Move Tool on the Edge of the Block

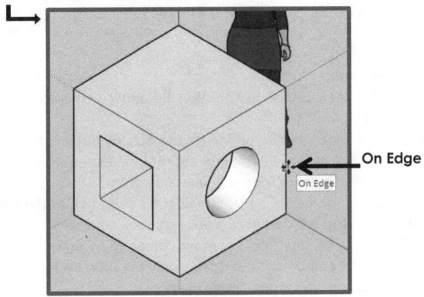

On Edge

- Click.
- Drag along the red axis line.
- Only the line selected is being moved, which has produced a distortion of the block. Obviously not what is wanted.

Only The Line Selected is Moved

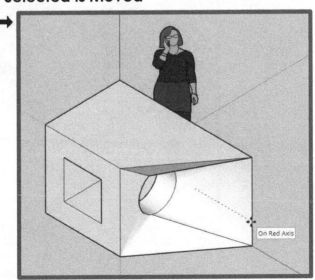

- Press the Escape Key.
- To move the Block all the entities must be grouped together.

To Create a Group

- Pick the Select tool and position the arrow on the right face of the block.
- **Press the pick button on the mouse quickly three times. This will select all the entities that make up the square block as indicated by blue lines and selection dots.**
- Another method is by positioning the **selection arrow outside of the top left corner** of the block and holding down the pick button on the mouse **move diagonally down to the bottom right corner** of the block so **only the block is inside the window frame** and then release the pick button.

Creating A Group

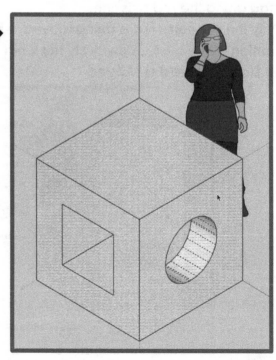

- Press the **Right button** on the mouse.

- This brings up the **Context menu.**

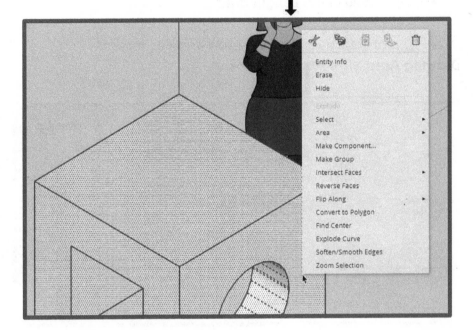

- Click the – **Make Group** – option.

- Now go and select the **Move tool.**
- Position the tool on the **Right face – 4 centre (ctr) marks** appear, along with the message – **On Face in Group.**
- **The 4 ctr marks are used if you want to swivel the block through an angle. The Protractor tool is displayed if you place the Move tool onto any of the ctr marks.**
- **Position the Move tool at the bottom right corner of the block – the corner that is on the Red axis line. The message – Endpoint in Group – appears.**
- **Click.**
- **Drag the block along the red axis in both directions – the whole block moves.**

- **Now move the block diagonally left along the red axis a message saying – On Red Axis - appears.**

- Type **1500** in the **Length area.**

- This produces a Drawing Area View as shown.

Drawing Area View

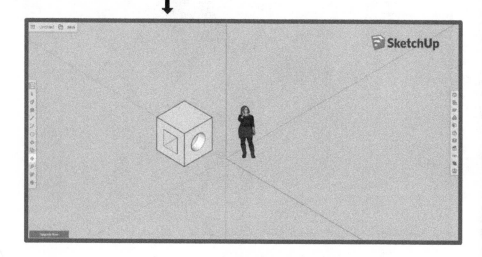

- **Press the Escape Key to complete the move.**

- **Now move the block so that the bottom right corner is on the origin point of the X, Y, Z axis.**

- Select the **Move Tool and position at the bottom right corner** of the block, the message - **Endpoint in Group**- appears.

- **Click and drag onto the origin point of the axis**

- Because you have grouped the block, all you have to do to move it, is **- indicate the base point and the destination point or type the distance the object is to be moved.**

- The position of the block is as shown.

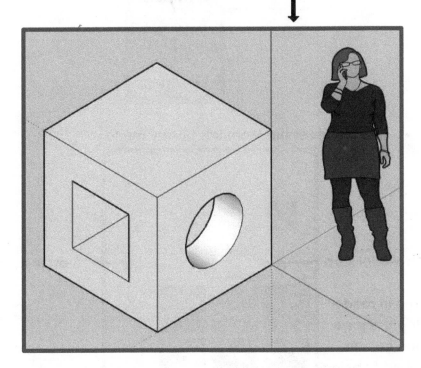

To group objects together

- Using the selection tool, pick the edges wanted or window the object or triple click the mouse button.
- Pick the Right button on the mouse – the context menu appears.
- Select the "Make Group" option.

How Do I Apply Colour and/or Materials

Being able to apply colour or material is an essential part of 3D Modelling. The colour or material applied transforms the model into a real looking object. To apply colours and materials you use the Materials Pane found in the Panels Bar on the right of the graphics screen. The Materials Pane contains a wide range of applications from paint to tiles to bricks and so on.

The Basics - Part One

- Select the Materials Panel in the Panel Bar.

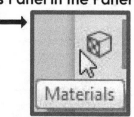

- This produces the Materials Library menu

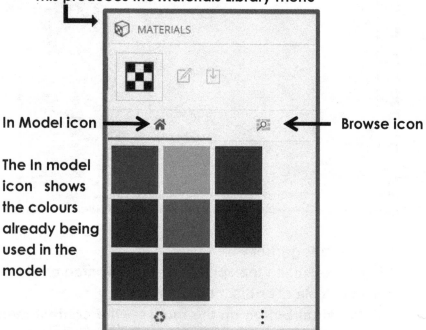

In Model icon

The In model icon shows the colours already being used in the model

Browse icon

The Browse icon shows the Varying materials and Colours available as shown on page 45

The Basics - Part One

Materials Library

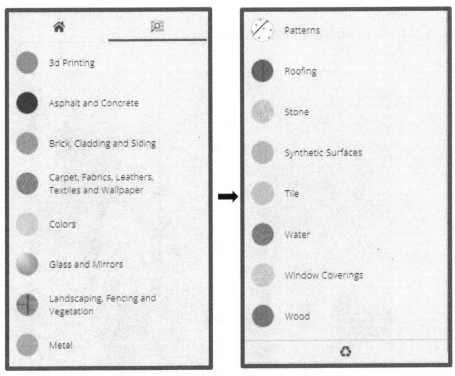

- Pick the **Browse Icon**
- Select - **Colors**.
- From the colour tiles displayed -
- **Click** the **Pink tile AO1** as shown -

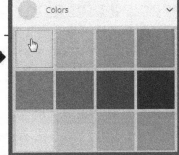

(The colour number is shown at the top Of the Materials menu) ➡

- Move the Paint Bucket tool on to the top of the block -
- Click.
- The colour chosen is applied to all, of the block.

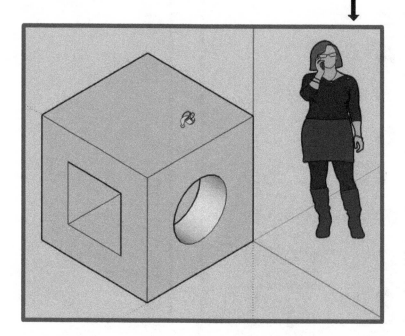

How do I Apply Colours and Materials to just a selected part of my object

You will find that on many models you only want to add colour or textures to certain parts of the model. Provided you haven't Grouped your model you can select any individual face and the colour or material will be applied to that face only. If you have Grouped your model, as we have, then you have to use the Edit Group option found in the Mouse On-screen menu.

- Close the Materials page.
- Pick the **Select tool** and position on the block.
- **Right pick on the mouse button – the group edges turn blue and the Context menu appears.**

- Highlight the - **Edit Group** - option and then – Click.

- **This produces what is known as a Bounding Box.**

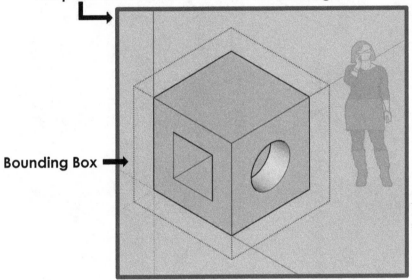

Bounding Box ➤

The Bounding Box indicates that you are going to edit the grouped object.

- **To change the colour on the face where the circular hole is -**
- Click the **Materials Panel.**
- The **Materials Library opens** at the same option that it was closed at.
- Select the colour tile – **C05.**
-

(The Letter A, B, C etc. Indicates the Row of the colour tile. Each letter is made up of two rows in descending order).

- Move the Paint Bucket onto the **Right Face** and **Click**.
- Only the Right Face gets covered in the new colour.

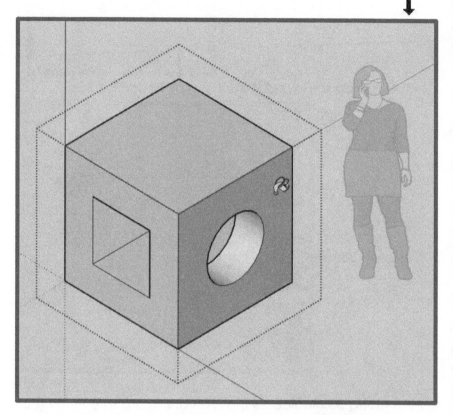

- **Notice the Bounding Box** is still surrounding the block to allow you to carry out further changes if required.

- Have a go at putting some other colours or other materials on the other faces.

- To remove the Bounding Box – Position the selection arrow outside the bounding box and Press the Right Button on the mouse and Click on the Close Group command.

- **On completion** put back to a **Perspective View.**

- **Zoom Window**

How Do I Save My Model

Having created our model the next step is in saving the model.

- Pick **Untitled** in the Home Toolbar.

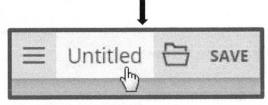

- **This takes you to your Trimble Account sign-in page.** Complete the Sign in procedure to verify who you are. This only happens the First Time you want to save your model.

The Basics - Part One

- You now have the **Trimble Connect Window Pane**

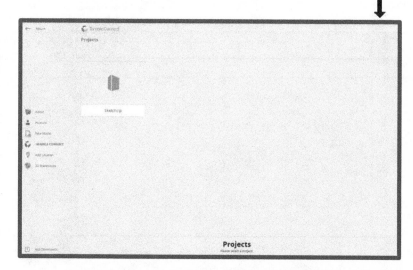

- Pick the **SketchUp Project box**

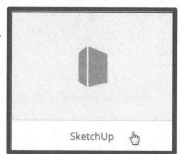

- **The Connect page shows the 3D model in the Project Box.**

- At the **Bottom of the Panel** you have the - **Name edit box.**

Name: Untitled

- Enter the name - **Exercise 1.**

- Pick the **Save here box**

Save here

The Basics - Part One

- The Name of the model - **Exercise 1. Skp** - is shown by the side of the 3D model in the Project Box.

Name Applied to the 3D Model

- Pick the **3D model in the Projection Box**
- Pick the **Open** button **in the Detail Pane** on the **Right of the screen.**
- **Close the Exercise 1 model.**

You now need to go and practice - So
- **Start SketchUp Free**
- In the **Opening Welcome Window** -
- pick **Create New**
- **From the options shown, select the - Simple Template - Millimeters**

- **Set the drawing environment -**
    - o **Set Model Info to the settings shown on page 26**
    - o **Parallel Projection**
    - o A - **Top View** - viewpoint.

In Exercise 1, we saved the model on completion. To see how to save the model after the setting of the initial environment -

- Pick **Untitled** in the **Home Toolbar**
- This produces the **Trimble Connect Screen.**

The Basics - Part One

- **Pick the SketchUp Project box**

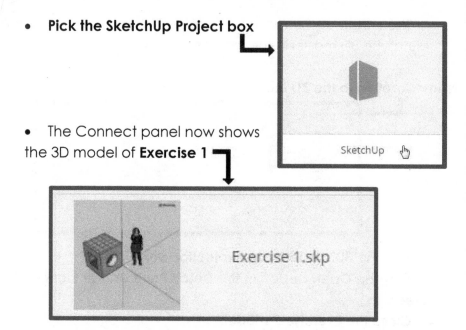

- The Connect panel now shows the 3D model of **Exercise 1**

- In the **Name edit box at the Bottom of the Panel,** type - **Practice 1**

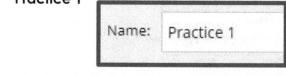

- Pick the **Save here box**

- **SketchUp then goes back to the SketchUp graphics screen and in the Home Panel you get the message - SAVING.**

- After a brief pause then the **name of the model with SAVED**

So you now have two ways to save your model. **I prefer this second method - save at the beginning of the modelling Project.**

- Using the methods shown produce a cube block that measures – 3000mm x 3000mm x 3000mm.

- At the centre of the left face of the block produce a 6 sided polygon hole which goes all the way through the block having a radius of 1000mm.

- In the centre of the Right face a Triangle that has a base

length of 2000mm and a vertical height of 1500mm that Extrudes out a distance of 1000mm.

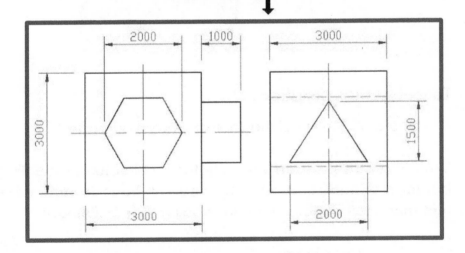

- On completion of the block

  o Put colours and materials on the varying faces.

  o Move the block so that the bottom right corner of the block – the corner that is on the Red axis line – is positioned at the Origin point.

  o Put Back to a Perspective View and then Close.

On completion, your model should be similar to that shown

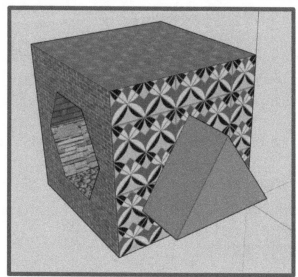

To get further practice;

Produce a 3D Model of the Casting shown on page 55.

SketchUp can be used not only for architectural modelling but for mechanical modelling. You just have to remember that mechanical parts are a lot smaller than buildings!!

- **Start SketchUp Free**
- In the **Opening Welcome Window** -
- pick **Create New**
- **From the options shown, select the - Simple Template - Millimeters.**

- **Set the drawing environment -**
  - o **Set Model Info to the settings shown on page 26**
  - o **Parallel Projection**
  - o A - **Top View** - viewpoint.

Casting Drawing

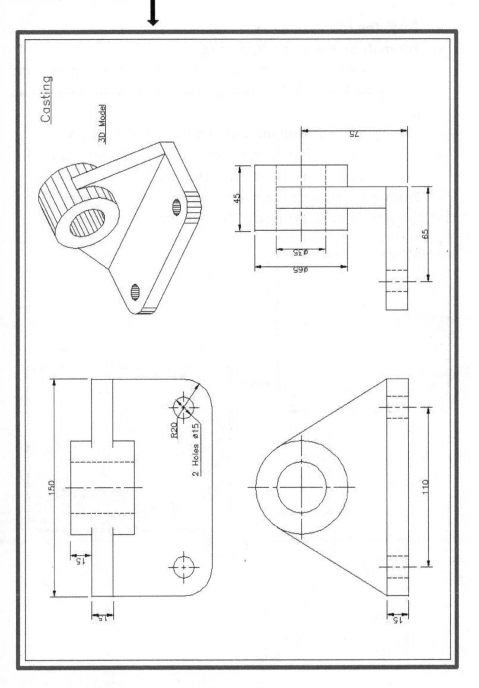

How Do I Produce the Casting

- **Erase the mannequin** (figurine).
- **Zoom IN on the axis origin point.**
- **Produce the base** by aligning the **front edge** so it **goes Right along the Red axis line 150mm and Up along the Green axis line 85mm.**
- **Change** your **viewpoint** and then **Push/Pull Up 15mm**
- Use the **Measuring Tool** to produce the **guidelines** for the **centres of the holes and 20mm radius.**
- **Produce** the **20mm corner radius** using the **Arc Tool.**

Using the Arc Tool To Produce The 20mm Corner Radius

- **Repeat for the other corner radius.**
- Use the **Push/Pull tool** to produce the **corner radius.**
- Use the **circle and Push/Pull tools** to produce the **two holes.**
- **Erase the guidelines.** ⌐

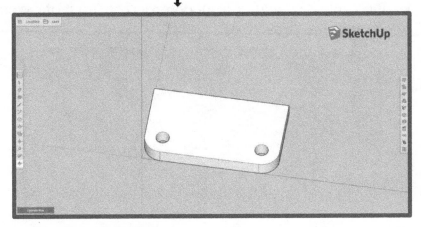

- **Make the base a Group**

To Produce the Vertical Support.

- Draw a **vertical line 60mm up from the midpoint of the back edge** of the base.
- Using the **Circle tool - position it at the endpoint of the verti-cal line (DO NOT PICK).**

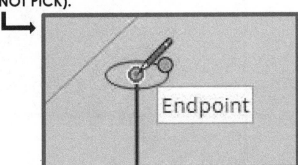

- **Notice** the Circle tool is **oriented in a Top Viewpoint which** means the **Push/Pull tool will only extrude in the direction of the Blue axis.**

- We need to change the orientation so the circle can be extruded along the Green axis - to do this - press the left directional arrow key on the keyboard. (Not the numerical arrow keys).
- **The circle** is now the **colour green** indicating that it is **orientated along the Green axis.**

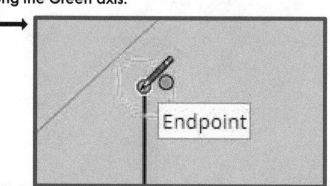

- **Pick the endpoint of the line** - produce the circle having a radius of 32.5mm
- Use the **Line tool to produce the shape of the vertical support** remembering that the **angle edges have to be tangential to the circle,** so **be careful where you pick.**

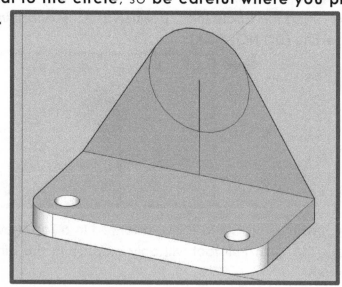

- **Complete** the vertical support and **then make it a Group**

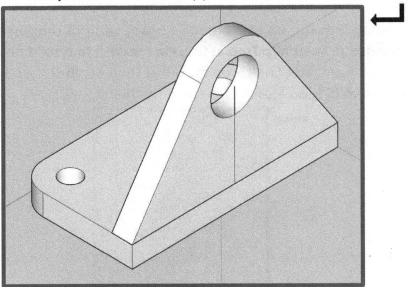

- Now produce the **Bearing Support Cylinder** – **Use the 60mm vertical line to help find the centre. Use the Move Tool to move into position – Remember to make the Cylinder a Group.**

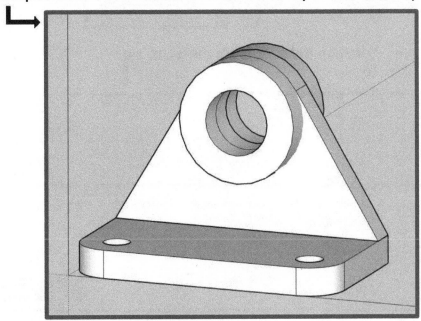

How Do I Make the Casting a Solid Object

The casting is made up of 3 groups – base, vertical support and the cylinder. In SketchUp Free to turn the model into a solid object.

- Pick the **Outer Shell icon** from the **Tools toolbar** then from the **group of tools** shown pick the icon - **Union**.

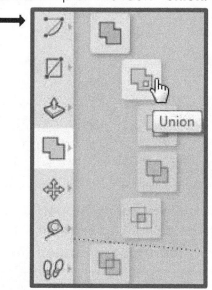

- **You then get shown this message**

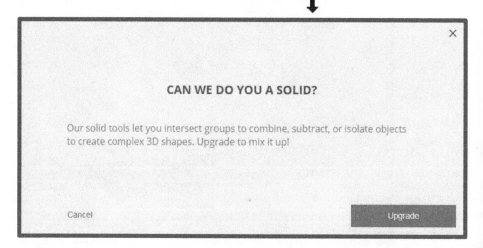

- **If you want to upgrade to another version of SketchUp you would pick the Upgrade button.** You are then shown the various SketchUp programs available indicating the price and comparison of functions.

- **As you do not want to upgrade, select - Cancel.**

- **This takes you back to the model.**

- **The selection arrow, which has attached to it, the solid/ non-solid symbol icon. This will indicate whether the object is solid or not. (The solid/non-solid symbol icon, is explained in greater detail in Part Two).**

- **Move the arrow onto the base of the casting and the symbol indicates that the base is solid.**
- **The 1 indicates the first object selected.**

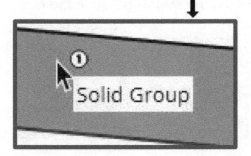

- **Press the Pick button** on the mouse.

- **Move** the **arrow onto the Vertical Support**

- **The number changes to a 2 indicating the Second object selected - Pick.**

- **Move the arrow onto the Cylinder and pick.**

- The three boxes merge into one.

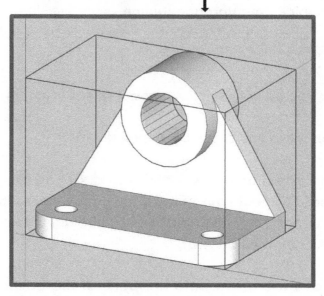

To make the casting more realistic, apply the material Aluminium Anodized from the Metals group in the Materials Library.

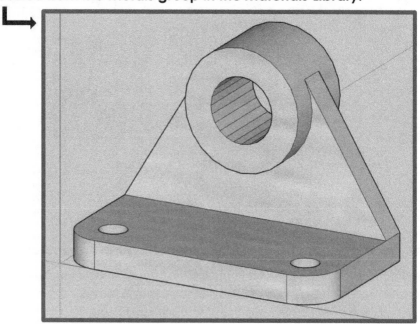

- Pick **SAVE** in the **Home Bar.**
- **Close SketchUp Free.**

Practice

As a beginner, to gain the skills to use SketchUp Free or any SketchUp program, you have to practice. The best way to gain the necessary skills is to practice what has been shown until you can repeat the processes without going back and having to see how to use this tool or that tool. You have to get to the level that you can produce the model by using only the information shown in the drawing. Before we move on, go back and produce the model of the casting by just looking at the drawing. Once you can produce the model without having to take sneaky looks you are ready to move on.

You need to DELETE the model of the Casting and to do that you need to gain access to the Trimble Connect Pane. At the moment all your models are saved in the Project Pane. To delete the Casting -

- **Start SketchUp Free**

- From the Opening **Home Sketchup Window pick - Trimble Connect.**

- Pick the **SketchUp Project box.**

- The **Connect panel** shows the **three 3D models** produced so far.

- Pick the **Casting.skp** and at the **right end of the bar pick the Delete (X) icon**

Selected Model

 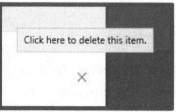

- You now get the **Please Confirm Message**

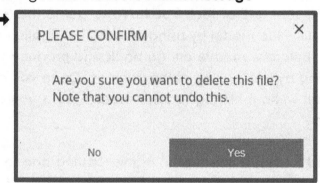

- Pick the **Yes Button.**
- You now have just the two models - **Exercise 1** and the **Practice 1 shown** in the **Connect Panel.**
  - Pick - **Return - up in the top Left Corner.**
  - You are **returned to the SketchUp Free Graphics Screen.**
  - **Close SketchUp Free.**

Repeat the methods shown in producing the Casting.
Remember to -
- **Set the Model Environment** by -
- Using the - **Simple Template - Millimeters**
- Use the **Model Info Panel** to set the - **Unit precision, Length Snapping and Snap Interval.**
- Change the View to **Parallel** and the **viewpoint** to **Top View.**

- **Save** the model as - **Casting** - by using the **Untitled option in the Home Bar.**
- **On picking save you are returned to the SketchUp Graphic Screen.**

- **Produce the Casting.**

SketchUp is used in producing 3D Models that are associated more with Architecture than Mechanical Engineering. To see how to use SketchUp Free on producing an architectural 3D model you can produce a simple model of a Dining Room having windows and doors along with furniture of a Dining Table and Six Chairs. The room layout is shown.

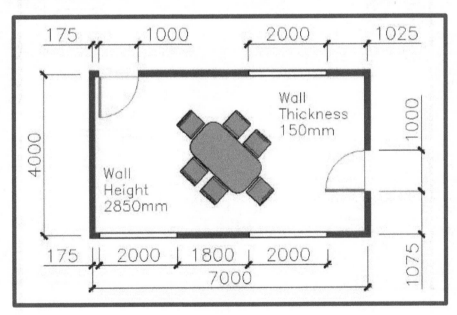

Measurements where appropriate are taken from the CENTRE of the walls

The Table and Chair sizes are shown on pages 66 and 67.

The Basics - Part One

The Furniture measurements are: Table

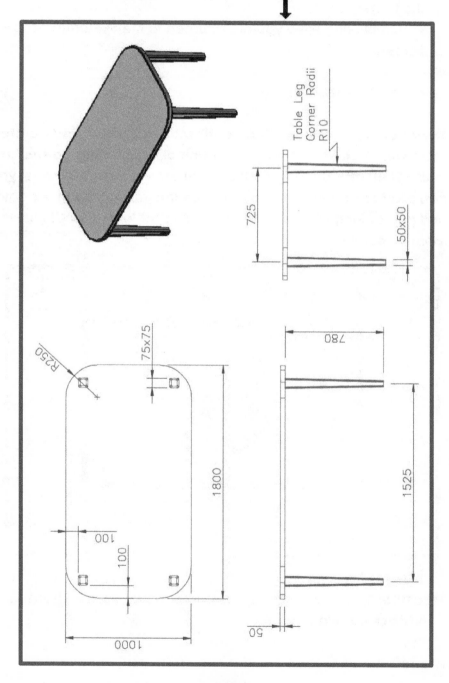

Chair.

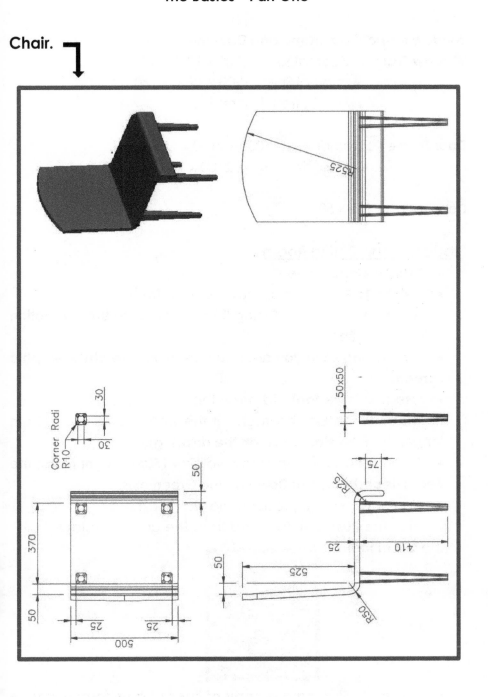

Window frame, Door frame and Door Measurements.

Window Frame – External Size = 2000 x 1300 x 150

Internal Size = 1900 x 1200 x 150

Height from Floor = 950

Door Frame – External Size = 1000 x 2150 x 150

Internal Size = 900 x 2100 x 150

Door – 900 x 2100 x 50

Producing the Dining Room

- **Start SketchUp Free**
- **Set the Environment** as shown earlier. Then -
- **Save** the model as - **Dining Room** - using the **Untitled option in the Home Bar.**
- **On picking save you are returned to the SketchUp Graphic Screen.**
- Use the - **Line tool** - to draw the external face of the wall (Remember the External faces of the walls are **75mm + 75mm longer than the stated size on the drawing).**
- External Face length of the walls = **7150mm Right along the Red axis and 4150mm Down on the Green axis.**
- You now need to produce the wall thickness.
- Pick the **Push/Pull** tool and from the group displayed pick the **Offset tool.**

- **This tool will create a copy of lines at a uniform distance either inside or outside of the selected lines.**

- Position the Offset icon on the face of the rectangle near one of the lines - You get the message - On Edge – Click.

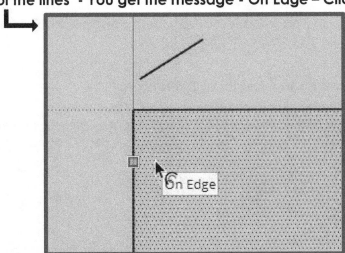

(If you move the mouse the lines are offset inward or outward).

- Move the lines inward -
- At the Distance edit box enter – 150.

- Adjust your view to a **Front-Right Iso.**

- Using the **Push/Pull tool - Extrude the walls 2850mm in height.**

Walls Extruded to a Height of 2850mm

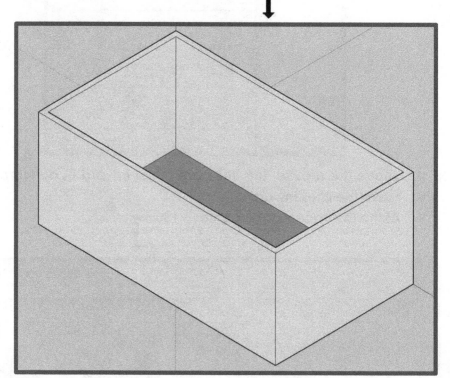

You now can put the openings for the windows.

- **Using the information given on Window Frames and from the Layout Drawing - put in the holes for the front window frames.**

- **Use the Tape Measure Tool to position the Guidelines and the Rectangle Tool to draw the outline of the window frame.**

- Produce the holes in the wall by using the Push/Pull Tool

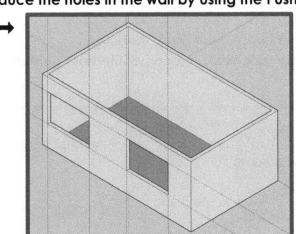

To create the window on the back wall –

- Move the guidelines 4000mm onto the inside face of the back wall by selecting the guidelines required.
- To position the guideline to help create the hole for the door frame - Move the front left vertical guideline 4000mm.

Guidelines moved onto the back wall

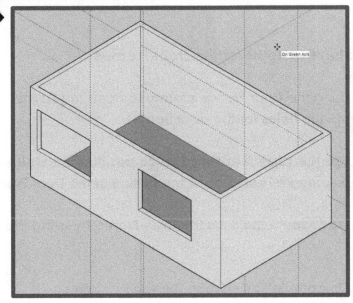

- **Orbit** the model so that the **guidelines are clearly** displayed.
- **Put in the hole for the back window.**
- **Erase the guidelines except for the door guideline**

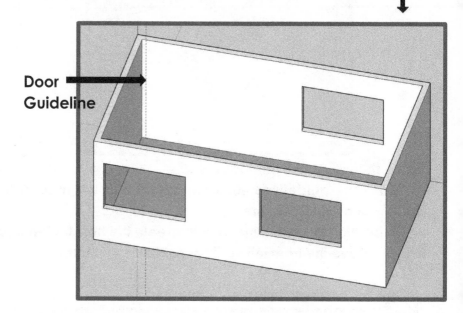

Door Guideline

Producing the Holes for the Door Frames

- Using the **Door Frame information** and the **Layout Drawing** – create the holes for the door frames.

- **Use the Tape Measure Tool to position the Guidelines and the Rectangle Tool to draw the outline of the Door Frame.**

- **Produce the hole for the Door Frame by using the Push/Pull Tool**

- **On completion – Group the walls together.**

Holes in The Wall Created for the Door Frames

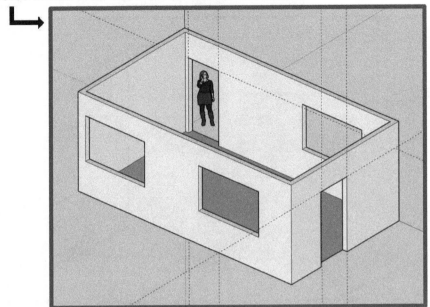

Creating the Window Frame

- **Erase the door guidelines.**

- Select the **Rectangle tool** and using the opposite corners of the **front left window opening - draw a rectangle.**

- **Repeat for the front right window opening.**

- **Offset** the **left window rectangle – 50mm.**

- **Repeat** by using the **INFERENCE** method on the **right window rectangle.**

How Do I Use the Inference Method

- **Click the bottom edge of the right window rectangle when** the message – **On Edge** – appears.

Offset Tool on the Edge of the Right Window Frame rectangle.

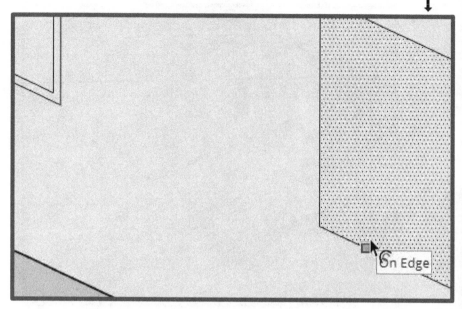

- Then go back and click on a point on the offset line in the left window rectangle.

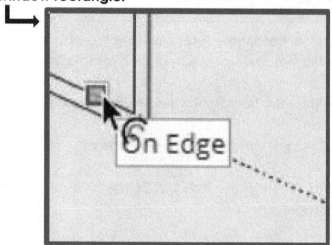

- This produces an offset in the right window rectangle at exactly the same distance as the original offset in the left window rectangle.

Using the Inference Method On the Right Window Frame

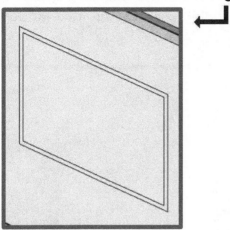

This method of Inference aligns an original object (this case the offset line in the left window) to the selected object (the right window) so that it is exactly in the same position and at the same distance as the original object. The Inference method can be used on other tools like the Push/Pull tool. (See later notes).

- Using the Select tool pick the inner area of the window frame then right pick on the mouse button and pick the erase option. Repeat for the other window frame.

- **This leaves the profile of the two window frames.**
- **Use the Push/Pull tool to produce the two window frames 150mm deep.**

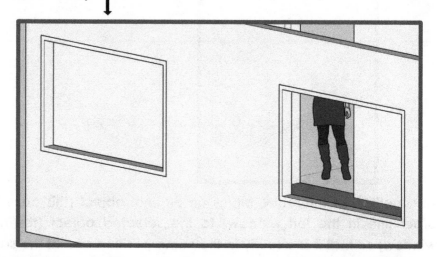

Creating the Third Window Frame will show you how to copy and create Components.

- To make copying the right window frame easier – **turn both window frames into Components.**
- Using the **select tool** – **window the left window frame** –

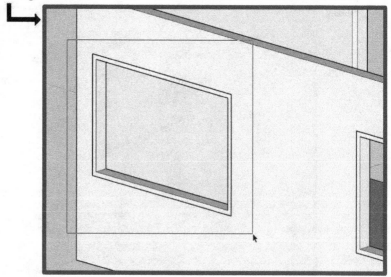

- **Then release.**
- The **edges and faces** that make up the window frame are **shown in blue**.

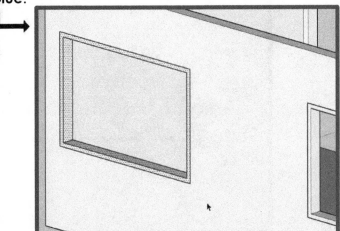

- **Position the selection arrow on the dotted blue surface and press the right button on the mouse and from the menu displayed pick the – Make Component – option.**

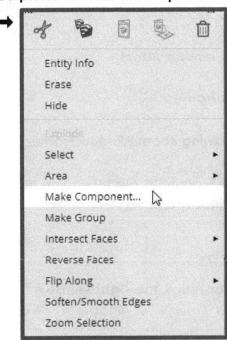

- In the **Definition** edit box type –
- **Window Frame 1.**
- In the Description Box - **Left Dining Room Window Frame.**

In the Alignment - **leave as None.**

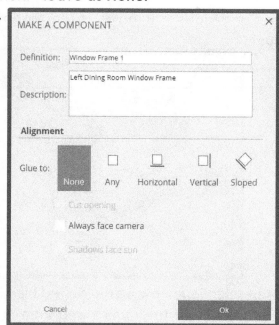

- Pick the **OK** button.

- **Repeat for the right window frame -**

- Definition - **Window Frame 2**

- Description - **Right Dining Room Window Frame**

- **Using the Orbit tool – orbit the model so you have a better view of the back window opening -**

How Do I Move & Copy

- Using the **Select tool pick the right window frame** – The **edges and faces** that make up the window frame **are shown in blue.**

Orbit to produce a better view of the back window opening.

- Select the **Move tool and position as indicated on the Right Window Frame.**

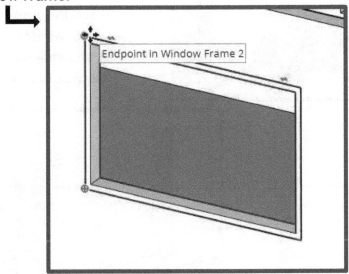

Endpoint in Window Frame 2

- **Holding the Pick button down** on the mouse – **start to move the window frame.**

- The **window frame is moved** from the window frame opening. ━━━━━━▶

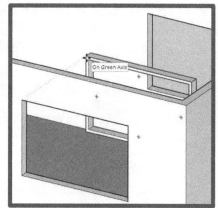

- **Still holding the pick button down – press the Control key (no need to hold the control key down).**
- **Pressing the Control key indicates you want to make** a copy of the selected component – notice that you now have two window frames, the original which has jumped back to its starting position, and a copy attached to the Move icon.

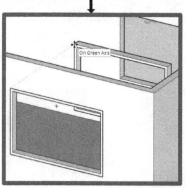

- **Move the copy onto the back window opening as shown – then Release the pick button.**

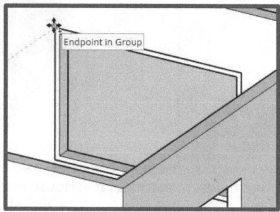

- Press the **Escape Key.**

- Change the viewpoint to a - **Front-Right Iso**
- **Adjust** the model **by - zooming and panning.**

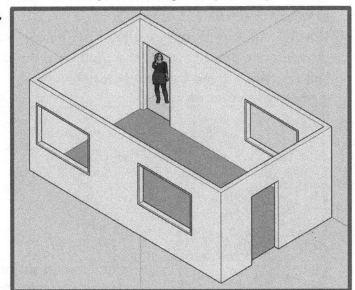

How Do I Produce The Door Frames and Door?

Using the information given on page 53, you can produce the two door frames and a Plain Door. But before proceeding in any production, put down how you are going to produce the object or objects required. This gives a guide, a sequence of operations that you can follow.

Action Plan
1. Start with the Right Wall Opening.
2. Use the Rectangle & Offset tool to draw the frame.
3. Extrude using the Push/Pull tool.
4. Group the Door Frame.
5. Copy the door frame.
6. Rotate the copied door frame using the Rotate Gizmo.
7. Move the rotated frame into the Back Wall Opening.
8. Produce one door – copy – rotate – move.

- Using the Line tool and the door frame opening in the wall, draw the external part of the door frame, then, offset 50mm to produce the inner frame.
- Create the frame by deleting the inner rectangle and drawing two lines down at the bottom of the original offset line and erasing the bottom rectangle.

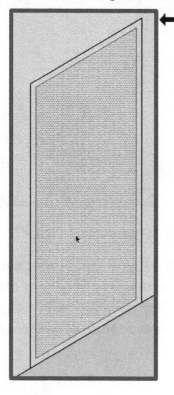

- **Push/Pull** to produce the **150mm** frame
- **Turn the frame into a Group**

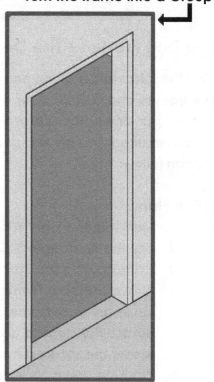

- Copy the door frame

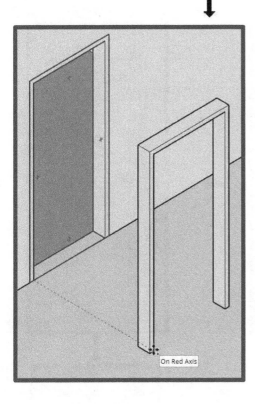

- Then on the copied door frame move the move tool to the top of the frame onto one of the red marks – the **Rotate Gizmo** appears.

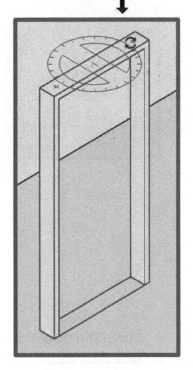

- Hold down the Pick button and start to rotate the door frame -

- it rotates at 15° increments –

- rotate until the dotted guideline aligns with the red axis.

- Release the Pick button and the door frame is as shown.

Rotating the Door Frame

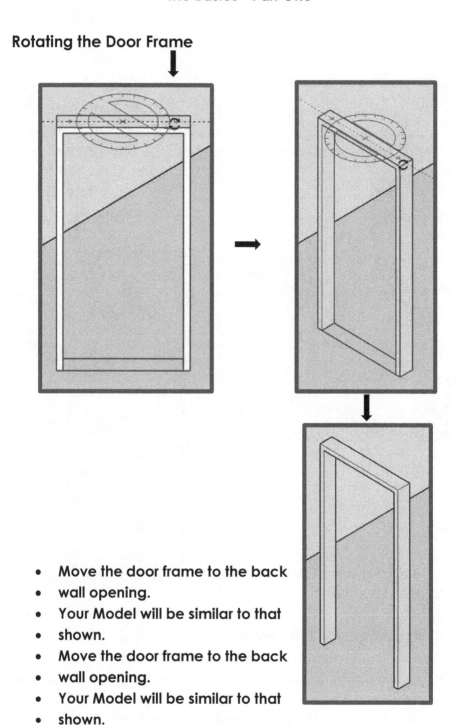

- Move the door frame to the back
- wall opening.
- Your Model will be similar to that
- shown.
- Move the door frame to the back
- wall opening.
- Your Model will be similar to that
- shown.

Your Model with the Window and Door Frames

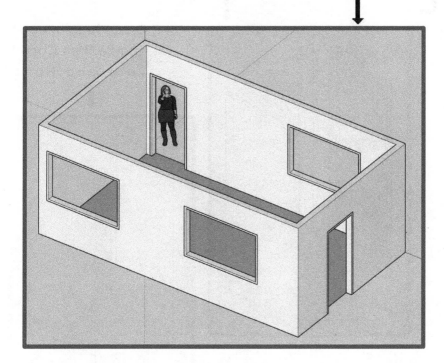

Produce the Plain Door –

- **Use the Rectangle tool & the Push/pull tool for the door.**

- **Move the door away from the door opening.**

- **Make into a Group.**

- Produce **guidelines to find the centre of the door handle,** which is **positioned 1150mm up from the floor and 100mm in from the edge.**

- **Produce a simple ɸ75x200mm door handle.**

- Make the handle **a Group** and **Move into position.**

Handle Moved into Position

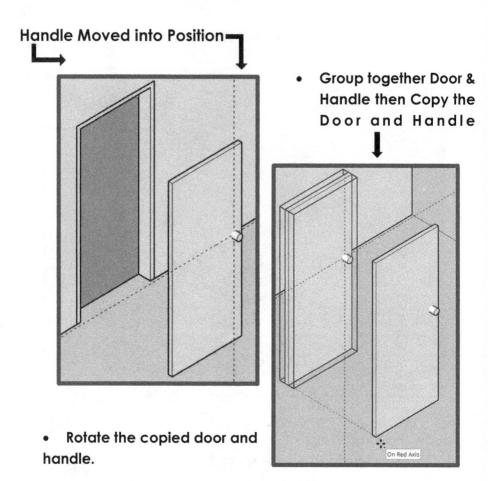

- Group together Door & Handle then Copy the Door and Handle

- Rotate the copied door and handle.

- **Use the Rotate tool** as you know how to use the Rotate gizmo.

- **Rotate Tool -**

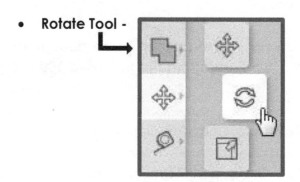

- **Position the Rotate icon at the midpoint - Pick.**

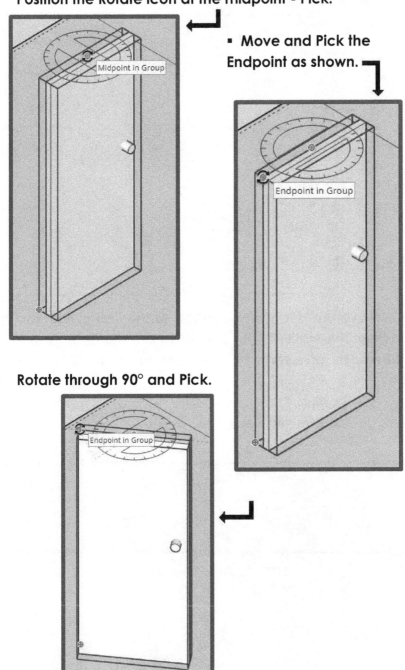

- **Move and Pick the Endpoint as shown.**

- **Rotate through 90° and Pick.**

- **This produces a view as shown.**

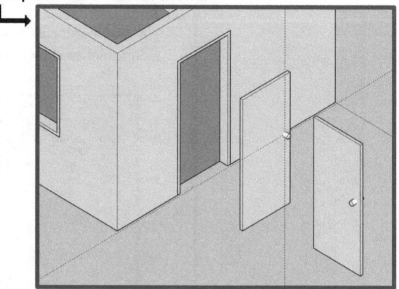

- **Move the doors into position so they align with the inside face of the walls.** You will have to **use the Orbit Tool and the viewpoint presets** from the View Panel **to help you align.**

- On aligning the doors use the viewpoint - **Front-Right Iso.** This gives a **Drawing Area View as shown -**

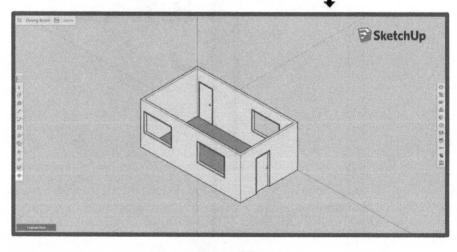

- The room is complete except, of course, for the furniture and applying materials.

- The applying of the materials can be done on completion of the furniture.

How Do I Produce the Table and Chairs

- Using the information shown in the table drawing, page 52, and the commands and techniques shown, produce the dining table.

- Start with the **table top.**

- Start the model **outside the dining room.**

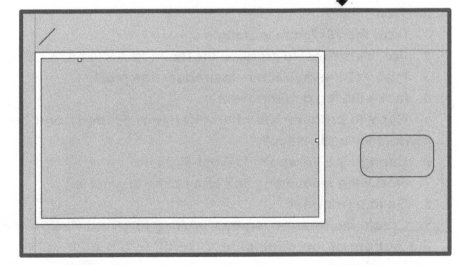

- **Move** the table **up 780mm**

- **On completion, it will look the same as that shown on page 90**

The Table Top

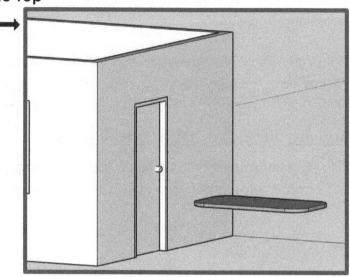

To Produce the Table Legs
Action Plan

1.   Draw the 75x75mm rectangle.
2.   Use the arc tool to produce the 10mm radius in each corner.
3.   Push/Pull the leg 780mm to produce the profile.
4.   Make the leg a component.
5.   Copy to produce the other three legs 500mm apart both horizontally and vertically.
6.   Change the Viewpoint to Front-Right Iso
7.   Producing a Bounding Box around the original leg.
8.   Go to a Front view
9.   Create the tapered leg by - orbiting to give a viewpoint of the bottom of the original leg - scroll to get a closer view.
10. Select the two arcs and the edge line at the bottom of the leg - hold the control key down when selecting the lines - they turn blue when selected.
11. Move the three lines in 12.5mm.
12. Repeat for the other three sides.

- **Following the Action Plan**

Action Plan 1 to 4

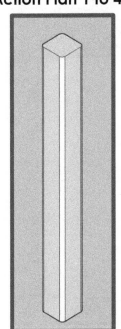

Action Plan 5

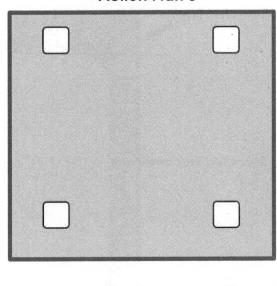

Action Plan 6 & 7

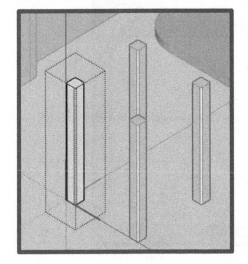

Action Plan 8

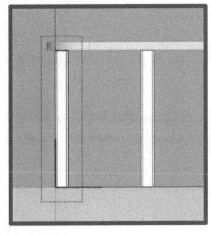

The Basics - Part One

Action Plan 9 & 10

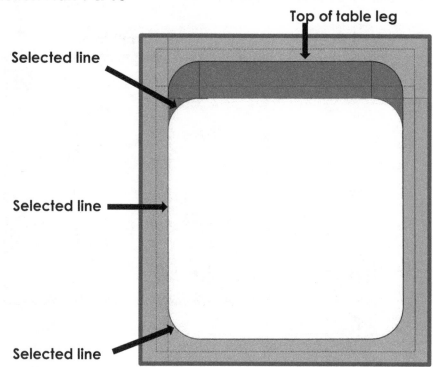

Top of table leg

Selected line

Selected line

Selected line

Action Plan 11

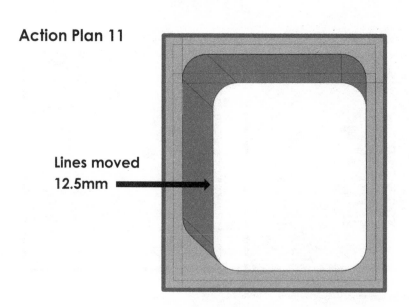

Lines moved
12.5mm

Action Plan 12

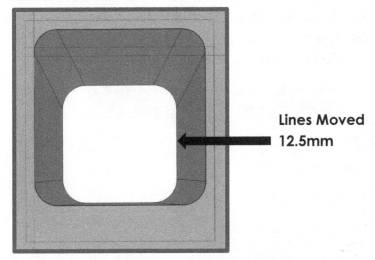

**Lines Moved
12.5mm**

- Scroll out until all four legs are displayed.
- You see that the changes done to the original table leg have taken place on the other three legs.

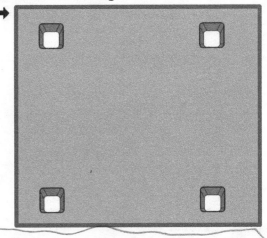

This change is the main difference between a Group and a Component. If you copy an object that is a component, any changes made later are reflected in all of the copied and original objects. Objects that have been Grouped and then copied, any changes have to be done on each individual copied and grouped object.

- **Move the legs into position – to help, put some guidelines on the bottom face of the table top as shown - then group the table top and legs.**

Use Guidelines to Position the Table Legs ⌐

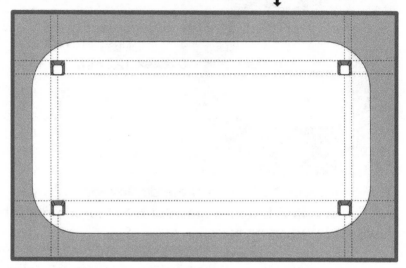

- On completion - **Go to a Front-Right Iso and orbit** ⌐

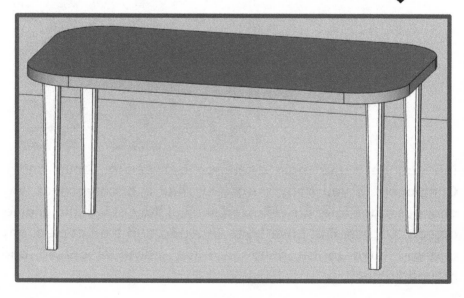

Producing the Chairs
Action Plan
1. Start in a Front View.
2. Draw profile of the chair seat and back.
3. Push/Pull.
4. Using the Arc tool put the radius on the chair back.
5. Push/Pull to produce the radius – erase any unwanted lines.
6. Group together.
7. Produce the chair legs – use a similar method as for the table legs.
8. Group together, the chair and the chair legs.
9. Apply Material to the Chair.

Action Plan 1 – 2

Action Plan 3

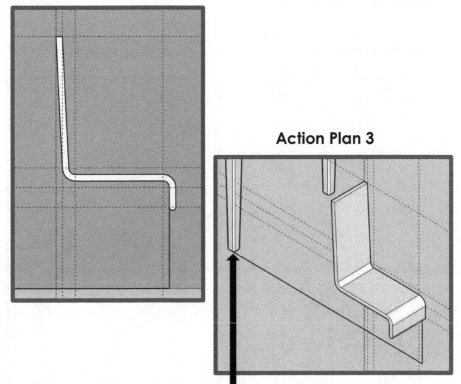

Baseline was drawn from the base of the Table leg.

Action Plan 4

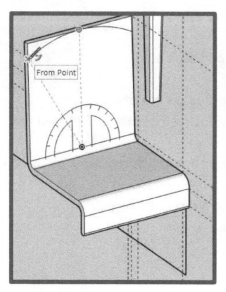

Action Plan 5 - 6

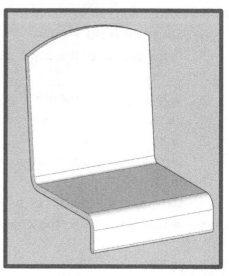

Action Plan 7 - 8

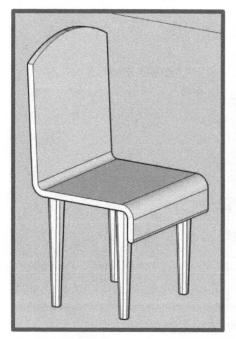

Action Plan 9

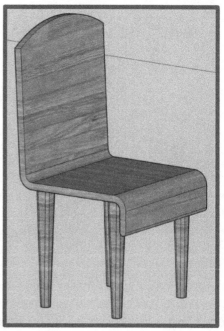

- **Having Produced the 1 chair you now need to produce the other five.**
- **Using the Move/Copy method - produce the other five chairs.**
- **To Rotate – Select the chair to rotate then use the Rotate tool.**
- Move the chairs into position around the table.
- **Apply a material to the table** - (It is a lot easier to apply materials to the table and chairs outside the dining room than it would be if they were inside the dining room).
- **Your table and chairs should be similar to that shown -**

Table and Chair Arrangement

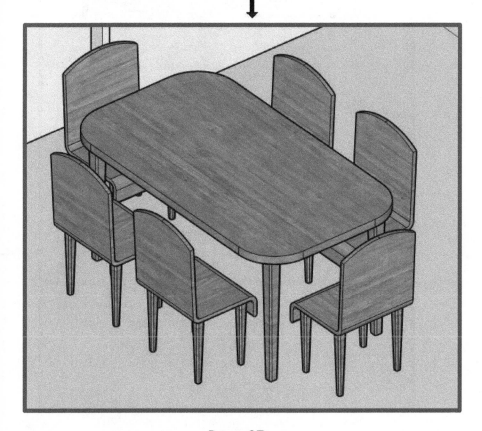

- Go and apply materials to –
  - Outside Walls
  - Inside Walls
  - Window Frames
  - Door Frames
  - Plain Doors
  - Door Handle
  - Floor – you will have to create the floor by using either the line or rectangle tool - use a floor thickness of 150mm.

- Arrange the table and chairs in the dining room.
- Your Dining Room will be similar to that shown below.

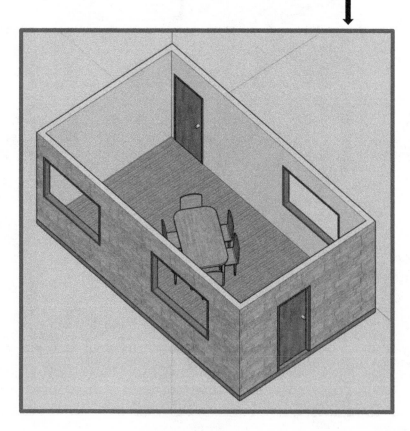

You now need to go and practice the commands and techniques that you have used in producing the Dining Room and furniture. Have a go at Project 1 – Bedroom Layout

Project 1 – Bedroom Layout

Project Details

In this project, you will learn how to use Layers and the Follow Me tool, how to revolve profiles as well as applying the tools and techniques shown.

Using the bedroom layout shown, produce a 3D model having windows and doors along with furniture of your choice but must include a bed, wardrobe, and makeup table.⌐

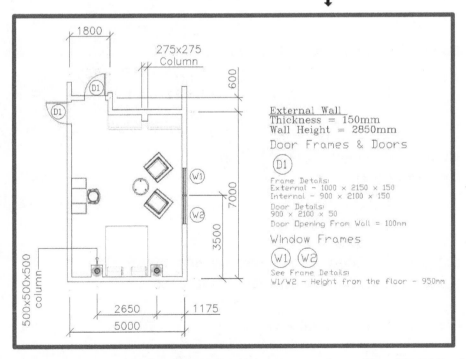

Measurements where appropriate are taken from the CENTRE of the walls.

Double Window Frame Details

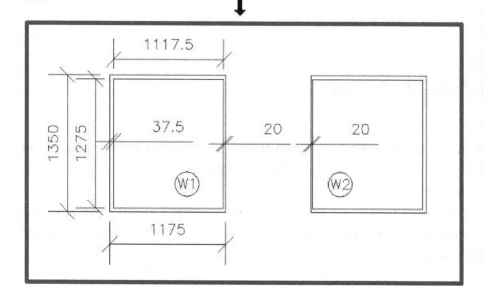

Double Window Frame – Single Frame Size -
>   Single External Size = **1175 x 1350 x 150**
>   Internal Size = **1117.5 x 1275 x 150**
>   Height from Floor = **950**

Window Casement (Casing) Details.
(See page 101).

Door Frame – External Size = **1000 x 2150 x 150**
>   Internal Size = **900 x 2100 x 150**

Panel Door – 900 x 2100 x 50

Panel Door Details.
(See page 101).

Window Casement Details

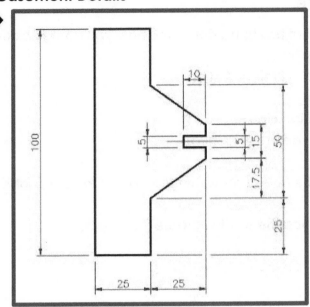

Panel Door Details

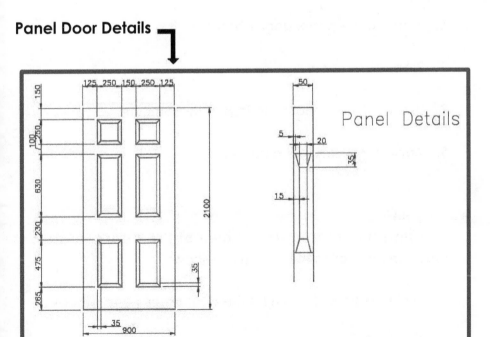

Panel Details

Procedure.

1. Study what has to be done and how you can go about doing it.

2. Start with a Project Action Plan.

General Action Plan
    1. Produce the wall layout.

    2. Put the holes (voids) in the walls for the doors and windows.

    3. Produce the window frame

    4. Produce the window casing

    5. Produce the door frame

    6. Produce the panel door + handles

    7. Produce the floor

    8. Use the 3D warehouse to import the furniture

    9. Apply materials to the model

Wall Layout
- Using the information shown of the bedroom layout produce the wall to the dimension shown.

- Put in the holes (voids) for the door frames and window.

- The model should look as in the **Drawing Area View.**

Drawing Area View ⌐

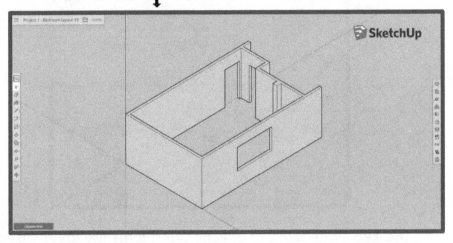

- Group the walls.
- Then put onto a layer called Walls.

How Do I Use Layers

- Layers are used to contain different parts of your model. The advantage of layers is that you can control what part of your model is displayed.
- Whatever object you put in the layer it <u>Must</u> be either part of a Group or a Component.
- ALL modelling should be done on Layer 0. This layer is the default layer which cannot be deleted or renamed.
    - To add layers you have to open the Layer Panel found in the Panels Toolbar
- From the **Panels Toolbar** – select the **Layer Panel** icon ➡

- **This Produces the Layers Panel**

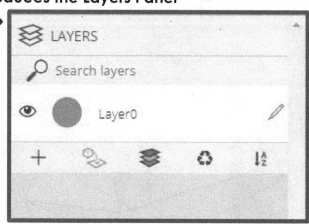

- **The Eye - checking or un-checking turns the layer On or Off. When checked (On), whatever is on the layer is visible, when unchecked (Off), it's not visible.**
- Next to the options button is the **Colour Disk. The colour shown is the colour that has been applied, by the program, to the layer. Every time you create a new layer the program will apply a colour to it.**
- **To change the colour you pick the colour disk.** This produces the **Select Layer Colour panel.**

- **By using the Slider, the Circular Pointer or the UP and Down arrow will let you select the colour for the current layer.**
- **The colour for layer 0 has been changed from Red to Blue**

- **The chosen colour of the layer is only displayed** on the model if the option - **Colour by layer** - is selected.

- **Click on the Color by layer option.**
- **The walls take on the colour of the colour disk.**
- **Go back and remove the check in the Color by layer option.**
- **Next to the colour disk, you have the layer name - Layer 0**
- **When producing a new layer by picking the + symbol, the name shown is Layer 1, pick again Layer 2 and so on. This is of very little use as you want the layer to reflect what is on the layer. So when producing new layers, type in the name of the group or component that is going on that layer.**
- **Click** on the **Plus symbol** and change the name to – **Walls**.

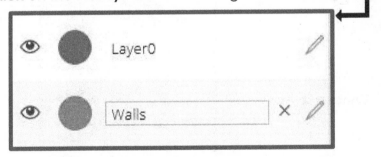

- **The Icon that looks like a pencil** indicates the active (current) layer.
- **You need to be careful because having another layer active other than layer 0 means whatever you draw is placed on that active layer.**
- **To gain access to a layer quickly it is best to have them arranged in alphabetical order. To do this you pick the Layers sorted in alphabetical order icon -**

Alphabetical order icon -

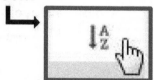

How Do I Put the Walls on the Wall Layer

- **Using the select tool select the walls,** then from the **Panels Toolbar** pick the **Entity Info** icon ➡

- This brings up the **Entity Info Pane** – **Which indicates the object is a Solid, its Volume, Colour, and the Current Layer.** ➡

- Pick **Layer 0.**
- This produces the **Choose Layer** Panel.

- **A list of layers is shown,** (at the moment just the two).

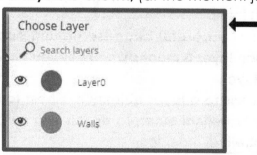

- Pick the **Walls Layer**
- The **Entity Info Panel is returned** indicating that the **Walls is** the current layer.

- **To check that the walls are on the walls layer -**
  - o **Close the Entity Info Panel**
  - o **Open the Layers Panel** and **turn Off the Walls layer**

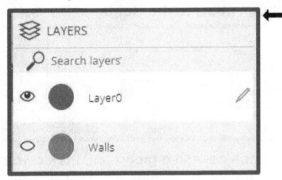

- **The model of the Walls disappears.**
- **As you need to be able to see the walls – make them visible again.**

You will create a number of different layers as the bedroom model develops.

Wall Layout Continued

- **Produce the 500 x 500 x 500 columns.**
- Use the **infer** method for the second column – **click the Push/Pull tool on the second 500 x 500 square rectangle.**
- Then - **move the Push/Pull tool onto the top of the first column and click. The second automatically infers to the height of the first.**

As shown on page 108

Push/Pull Tool Positioned on the second column

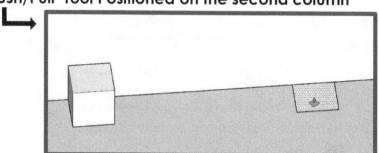

Second column infers to the Height of the first column.

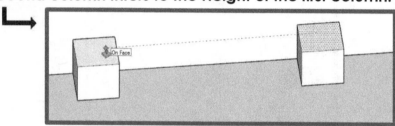

- Make each column **a group** and then **create a layer - Mini Column** - put each column on to the Mini Column Layer through - Entity Info.

With the wall and mini columns complete, you can now concentrate on the windows and doors.

How Do I Produce the Window Frames and Casements

Action Plan

1. Draw one frame, copy and revolve so the 20mm part of the frame is on the inside.
2. Draw the profile of the casement (casing) and position at the centre point of the frames.
3. Using the Follow Me tool produce the casement.

4. Group each individual window frame.

5. Put the two frames together.

6. Union to make one solid.

Action Plan 1 - Window Frame

You can construct the window frames within the window opening in the wall or make the Wall and Mini Columns layers invisible and construct the window frames as separate entities as shown.

- Turn the Walls and Mini Column layers OFF
- Produce Window Frame 1.
- Copy to produce Window frame 2
- **Remember** the inner vertical parts of the frames are only 20mm wide which means you will have to **revolve window frame 2.**
- Revolve

Window Frame 1 Copied and Revolved

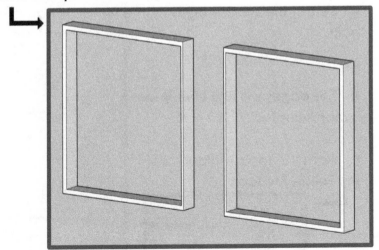

Action Plan 2 - Window Casement

- **Go to a Top View** and draw the **casement profile.**
- Copy the profile.
- **Orbit and then move into position, use a guideline to help position the profile.**

Positioning the Casement Profile

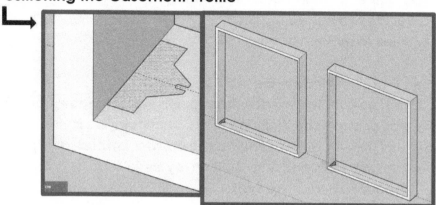

- **Repeat for the second frame.** ⌐

Action Plan 3 - The Follow Me Tool

- **The Follow Me tool requires a Path or Face to follow.**

- **Select the inner edges** of the window frame **to create a path.**

- The **edges will turn Blue** When selected.

- From the **Tools Toolbar,** pick the **Follow Me Icon**

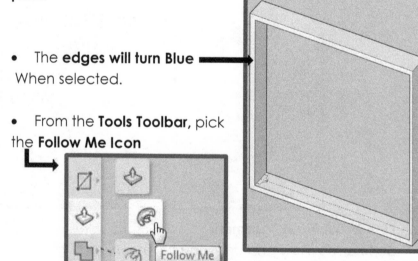

- **Position the Follow Me Tool over the casement profile as shown on page 111.**

The Follow Me Tool positioned on the Casement

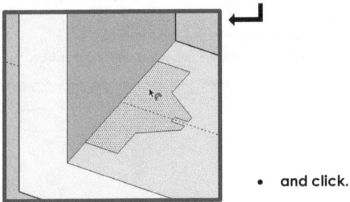

- and click.

- The profile follows the direction of the path to produce the casement.

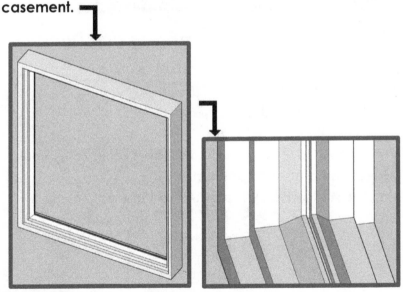

- Repeat for the second frame.

Action Plan 4, 5 & 6

- Make a Group of each individual window frame.
- Put both frames together so they look like one large frame.
- Union the frames together so they become one individual window frame.

- **Create a Windows layer** and then **use the Entity Info to put** onto this layer.
- **Turn ON the walls and minicolumns layers.**
- **Using the Move tool – move the window into position.**

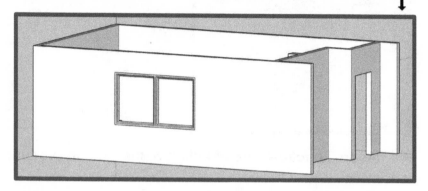

How Do I Produce the Door Frames and Door

Action Plan
1. Produce a door frame using the sizes given.
2. Then group, copy and rotate.
3. Create a door frame layer
4. Put the two door frames onto this layer using Entity Info
5. Move the frames into position.

Following the Action Plan will produce a View as Shown -

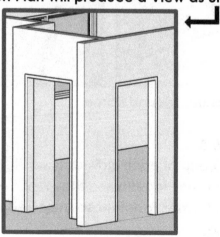

The Basics - Part One

To Produce the doors –

Action Plan

1. Produce a plain door using the sizes given
2. Use guidelines to help position the door panels
3. Produce the outer edges of the panels.
4. Create the holes for the panels.
5. Produce the Profile of the panels.
6. Place Profiles in the holes.
7. Produce Panels using the Follow Me tool.
8. Erase the vertical line in the Panel.
9. Group and Put on Door Layer.
10. Produce Door Handle
11. Place door handle in position
12. Copy, Rotate and place doors in the door frames.

Following Action Plan 1 - 3

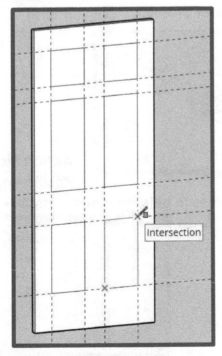

Action Plan 4 - Producing the Holes

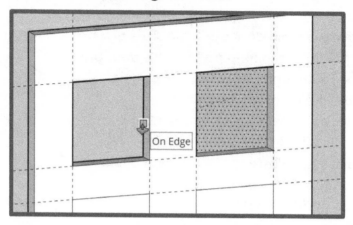

- Create the hole where the panels are to go – use the infer method to save having to type 50mm each time.
- Remove the guidelines for the door.

Action Plan 5 - Panel profile.

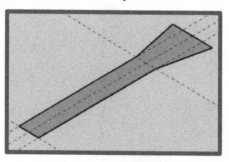

Action Plan 6 - Positioning the Profiles

- Put in Guidelines to help position the profiles

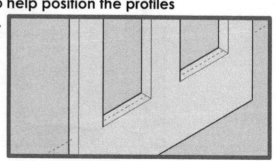

- Then - **Position the profiles.**

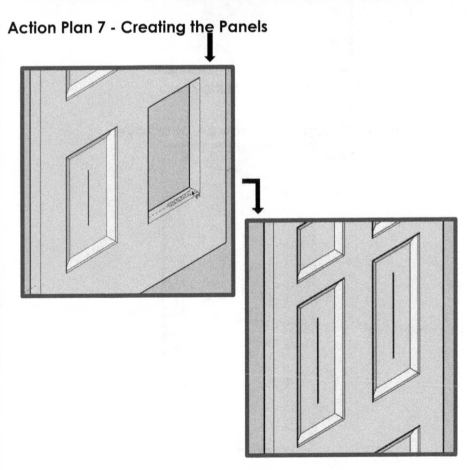

Action Plan 7 - Creating the Panels

Action Plane 8 - Erasing the Panel Line & Dots

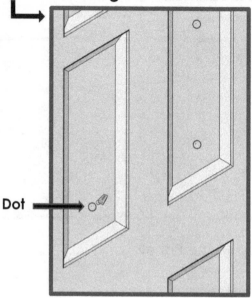

Dot ➡

- Repeat for the other side of the door.

Action Plan 9 - Group and place on Door Layer

Action Plan 10 - The Door Handle

- Use the following information to create the door handle.

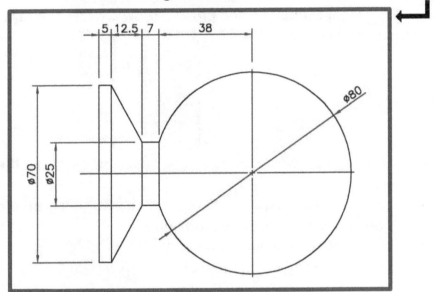

- **Make** the **Door invisible** by picking the **Eye icon** from the **Layers Panel.**
- **Make** the **Top View current.**
- Start at the **origin point of the axes**
- Use **Guidelines, Circle and Line tool** to draw the profile – then **erase the bottom half of the profile.**

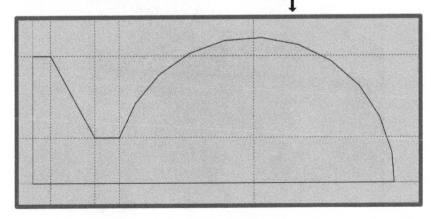

- **Erase the Guidelines**
- Change the viewpoint to **Front-Right**
- At the **Right Endpoint of the profile** – Draw a circle 50mm in diameter on the Red Axis. ➡

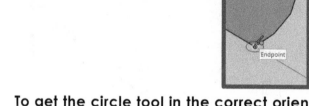

- To get the circle tool in the correct orientation along the **Red Axis**
  - **Position the blue circle tool at the end of the profile and press the Right Direction arrow.**
  - The **circle colour changes to Red Indicating** the **circle tool** has been **Orientated along the Red Axis.** ⬎

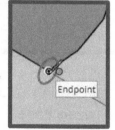

- **Pick -**
- **Draw the 50mm diameter circle.**

50mm Diameter circle drawn at the right end of the profile ⬎

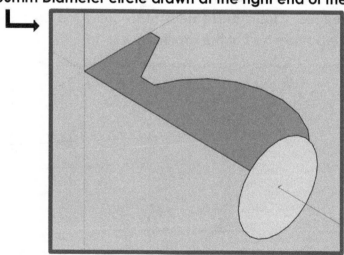

- Move the circle 50mm to the Right parallel to the Red Axis – you get a message saying On Red Axis.

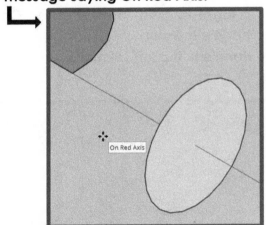

- To **REVOLVE (Lathe)** the Profile, use the **Follow Me** tool.
  o Click on the **Follow Me tool and position within the Handle Profile and then Click**
  o **The profile is revolved.**
  o The **Follow Me tool automatically follows the circular path of the moved circle.**

Automatic Rotation of the Handle Profile

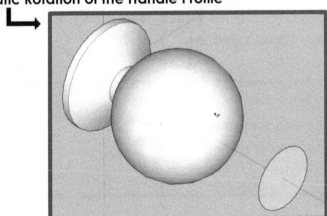

- **Erase the Circle.**

To Produce a Second Handle

- Go to a **Top View**
- **Pan** to the **Right** to give some room to **Copy and Flip.**
- Make the handle **a Group**
- **Copy the Handle to the left 150mm**

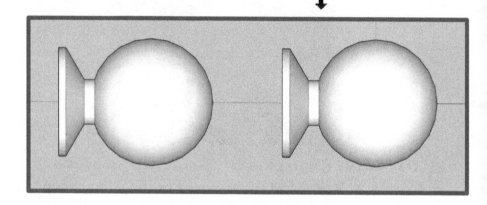

- **Put both Handles onto a Handle Layer**

- **To Flip –**
    - o **Use the selection tool and select the handle on the left**
    - o **Press the Right button on the mouse and from the options displayed select - Flip Along and then choose the – Group's Red.**

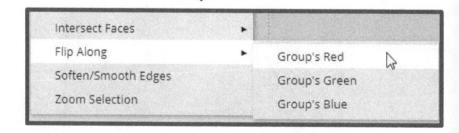

The left handle gets flipped along the Red axis.
(See page 121)

Left Handle Flipped ⌐

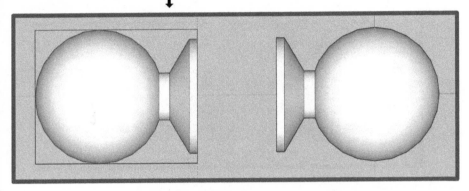

- **Adjust the gap between the handles to 50mm by using the Move tool.**
  - ○ Move together ⌐

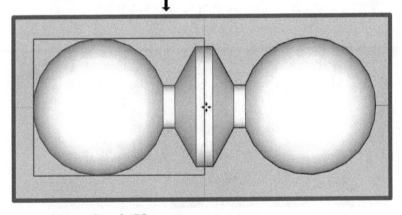

  - ○ Move Back 50mm ⌐

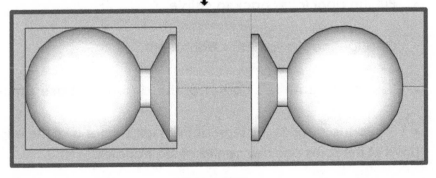

○ **Check with the Measuring tool**

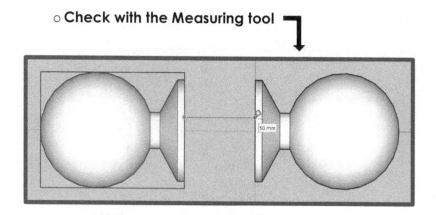

Action Plan 11 - Putting the handles in position on the Door

- **Move both Handles 50mm to the Right**

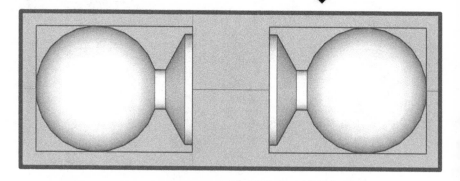

- **Put the Door layer back to visible.**

- Change the viewpoint to **Front-Right**

- Use the **bottom left corner of the door as a base point** –

- Move the door so that the **bottom left corner is at the origin point of the axes and the centre of the handles.**

Position of the Door and Handles ⌐

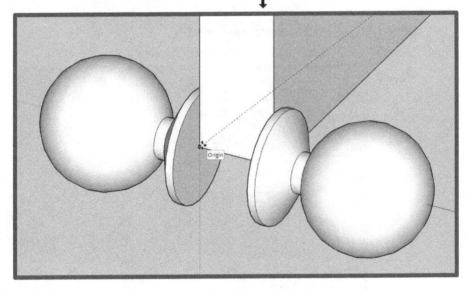

- Now move the handles **In 75mm (Green Axis)** and **Up 1150mm (Blue Axis)**

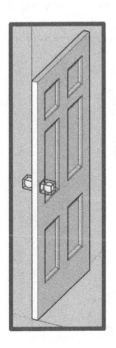

- **Copy the door and handles using the Green axis as a guide,** then **Rotate** the copied door and handles.

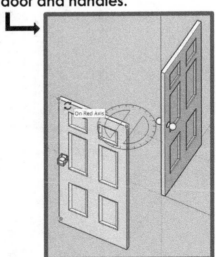

Action Plan 12 - Putting the Door and Handle in Position in The Door Frame

- Make the layer **Door Frame - Visible.**
- Move the doors into an **approximate position** then -

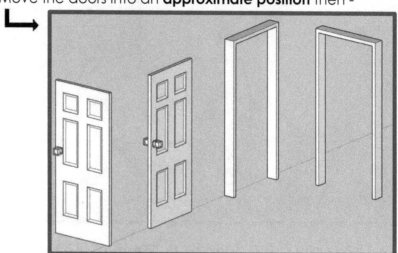

- **Move the doors into position** – Move to the **inside of the Door Frames.**

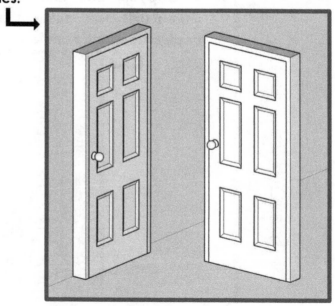

- **Open the Layer menu and make All of the layers – Visible.**

- This produces a **Drawing Area View** as shown.

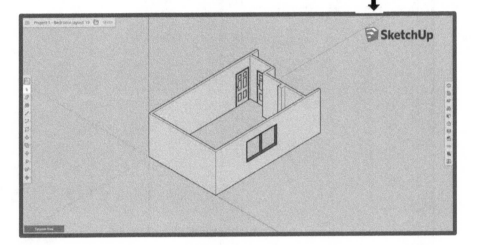

How Do I Create a Floor

- **The floor needs to be 500mm bigger from the outside of the walls and 150mm deep.** This type of floor is known as an **Apron Floor.**

- Set a **Top Viewpoint**

- **Use the rectangular tool starting from the bottom right corner to the top left corner of the walls.**

- **Offset** the rectangle **500mm.**

- **Make the walls invisible.**

- **Erase the Inner Rectangle.**

Walls Viewed in a Top View Point (Plan)

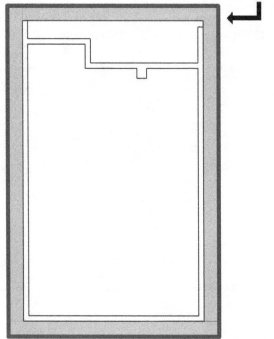

Inner Rectangle Erased

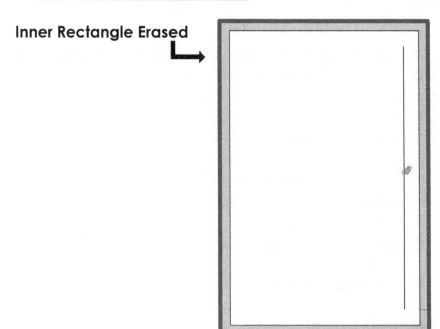

- Change the viewpoint to **Front-Right Iso.**

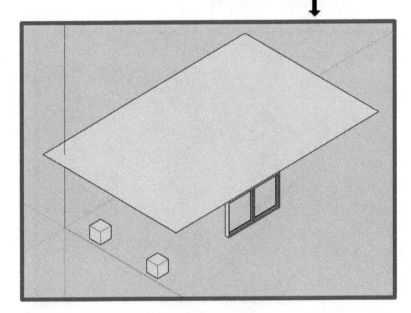

- **Move the floor area down 2850mm.**
- **Using the Push/Pull tool pull the floor area down 150mm**

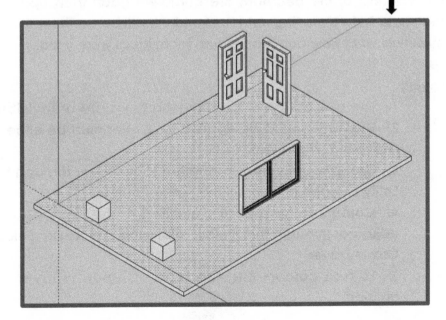

- Make the viewpoint - **Back-Right Iso current**
- **Make the walls Visible.**

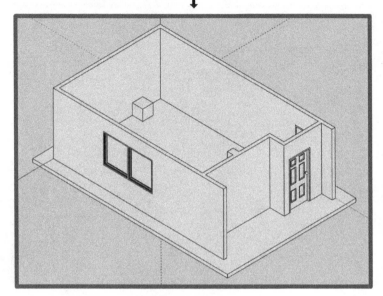

- Get back to a **Top viewpoint.**

The Exteriors of the bedroom are complete apart from applying materials. Before moving onto the interior it will be worth reminding ourselves what new commands and techniques were used.

Layers

1. The use of layers to make parts visible or invisible.
2. That any part to be applied to a layer must be either a Group or Component.
3. Group/Component Is applied to the layer through the Entity Info option found in the Panels Toolbar.
4. Colours automatically applied to the layer can be adjusted through the Colour disk and The Layer Select. Colour panel.
5. To turn colours ON, the icon - Colour by layer - is applied.

The Basics - Part One

Follow Me Tool

1. The Follow Me tool is used when a shape/profile needs to be duplicated along a given path.
2. Draw the Shape/Profile, place in position, indicate the path.
3. Select the Follow Me tool and place on the face of the shape/profile – click.
4. The shape/profile is duplicated along the selected path.

Revolve

1. To revolve a shape/profile, a circle and the Follow Me tool are used.
2. Produce the shape/profile to be revolved.
3. Draw a circle that is 90° to the profile.
4. Select the Follow Me tool and click on the face of the shape/profile.
5. Or. Move the Follow Me tool onto the edge of the circle and follow the edge until the shape/profile is closed.

Flip – Mirror

1. To reverse an object the Flip Command is used.
2. Select the object to Flip.
3. Right click on the mouse button.
4. Select the option, Flip Along – select the colour axis.
5. To Mirror an object –
6. Copy the object then select the copied object
7. Right Click – select the option, Flip Along – select the colour axis

Tape Measure Tool / Guidelines

1. Though not new, it is worth remembering the importance as to the use of guidelines and the use of the Tape Measure Tool.

2. Throughout a project's development the tape measure tool is used con-stantly, whether for positioning objects or for measuring.

How Do I Produce the Bedroom Interior

To complete the bedroom the furniture has to be put in. You could have-a-go at designing and producing your own furniture, but at this stage, why bother when there is a whole warehouse full of furniture.

- To import furniture you use the 3D Warehouse option found in the - **Components Pane** in the **Panel Bar**.
- **Open** the **Components Pane** by picking the - **Components icon**

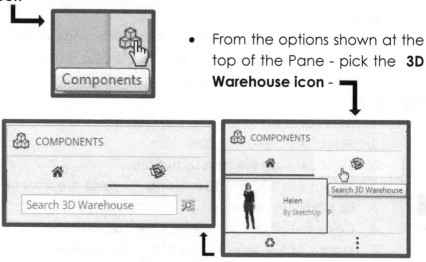

- From the options shown at the top of the Pane - pick the **3D Warehouse icon** -

- The, Search 3D Warehouse box is where you type what it is you want to import into your model.
- Let's start off by importing a King size bed.
  - o In the search box type **King Size Bed.**
  - o Pick the **search icon** at the side of the box.

o This produces the **1st page of 52pages** showing 3D Models of King Size Beds.

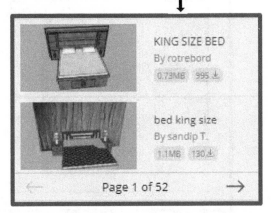

- **Scroll through to preview some of the beds available.**
- **The image shown gives you re-lated information including the name of the person who cre-ated it, its size and the number of downloads.**
- **On finding a bed - click on its image - a download message appears.**

  o **Drag into the bedroom** as shown in the **Drawing Area View.**

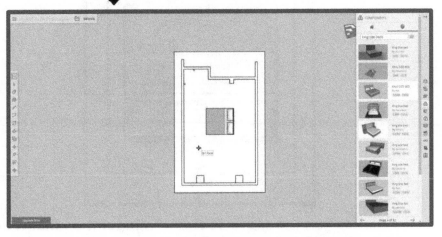

(The bed I am using is a King Size Bed created by Dee)

o Pick – **the blue selection box surrounds the bed**

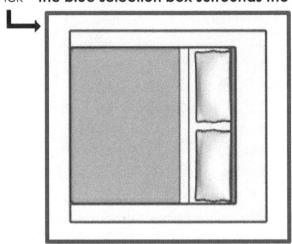

- **To position the bed so that the headboard will be against the wall and between the 500mm columns -**
  - o **Position the Move Tool on one of the red marks –**
  - o The **Rotate gizmo** is displayed –
  - o **Pick and rotate through 180°.**
  - o **Pick**

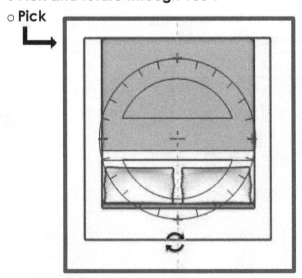

  - o Position the M**ove Tool** at a **midpoint on the head-board- pick.**

o **Move to the midpoint on the wall between the two 500 x 500 columns - pick**

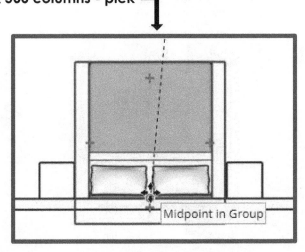

- **Create a layer named Bed and using the Entity Info put the bed onto the Bed layer**

- You now need to **check** that **the bed is sitting on the floor** after moving it into position.
- **Set to a Right viewpoint**
- Make the **Walls Invisible**
- **As can be seen, the bed is hovering some way above the floor.**

Positioning The Bed

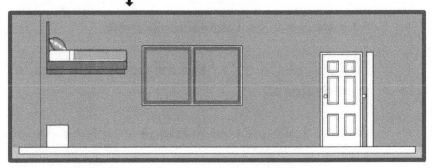

- **To move the bed down –**
  - o **Use the orbit tool to give you a 3D viewpoint.**

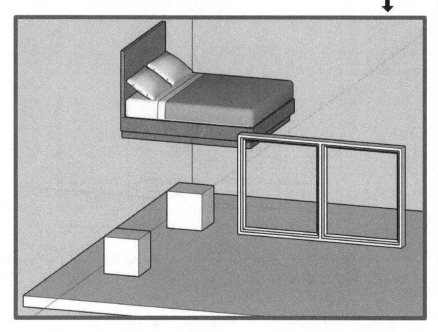

  - o **Select the bed** – the blue selection box surrounds the bed.

  - o Pick the **Move tool** and **position on the base of the bed**, the message – **On Edge in Group** – appears.

  - o Click

  - o **Slowly move the bed vertically down.**

  - o As you move down **the message – On Blue Axis – should appear.**

  - o Move down until **the message – On Face – appears, then –**

Bed Moved Down on to the floor

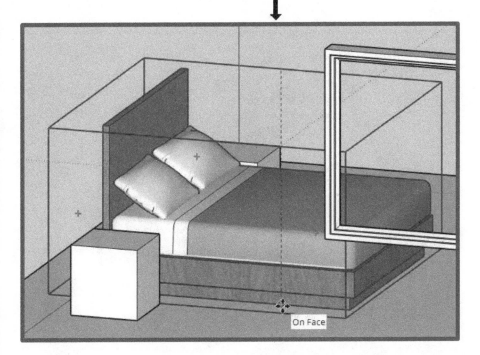

o **Click and remove the blue selection box.**

Importing the Remaining Furniture

- **You now need to complete importing the remaining bed-room furniture – remember to put them onto their own layers.**
- Also **import other objects** such as **bedside lights, a coffee table and a couple of easy chairs for example,** not just the bed, wardrobes, and dressing table.
- **Your Bedroom will look very similar to the one shown on page 136**
- **Save your model** - the Home bar will show **Saved** once the model has been saved.

≡ Project 1 - Bedroom Layout 🗁 SAVED

- **Close SketchUp**

The Bedroom with Furniture

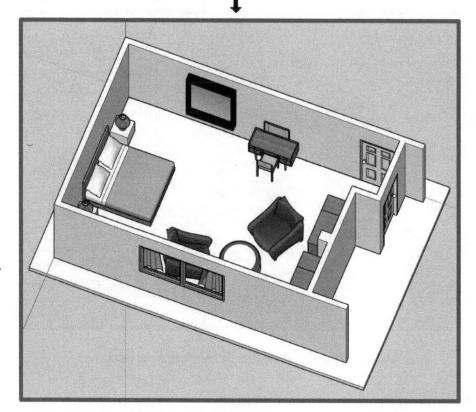

You still have to **apply Materials to the walls and floor.** Before doing that, let's see how to **Open a Model and create your own 3D Warehouse.**

How Do I Open a Saved Project

- Start **SketchUp Free.**
- **In the SketchUp Home Opening Window you have displayed your recent models.**
- **Double Pick** the **Project 1 - Bedroom Layout.skp**
- After a few seconds, the **Project 1- Bedroom Layout** model **is displayed in the Graphics Screen.**
- You can now continue to develop the model.

If you cannot see your model.
- **Down the left hand side of the SketchUP Home Opening Window, Pick the - Trimble Connect - Option.**
- **This puts you into the Trimble Connect Project Window.**
- **Pick the Project Icon.**

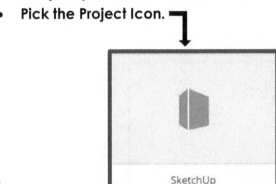

- **From the list of Projects displayed select the model wanted,** let's say, **the Project 1- Bedroom Layout.**
- Down the **right-hand side of the graphics screen** is the **Details Panel** which **gives information about the selected model.**
- Pick the **Open button** at the bottom of the Details Panel.
- After a few seconds, the **Project 1- Bedroom Layout** model **is displayed.**

As mentioned earlier, materials need to be applied to the walls but it would be a good idea to see how to create your own warehouse. Having your own warehouse containing models that you use frequently avoids having to go to the 3D warehouse and trying to remember on what page is the required model.

How Do I Create My Own 3D Warehouse

- Click on the **Open Model/Preferences** icon in the **Home Bar**
- **Assuming you used the first method of Opening a Saved Project** - This takes you back to the **Home Opening Window.**

- Down the Left side, Pick the Trimble Connect option.
- This puts you into the Trimble Connect Project Window.
- If you use the Second method of Opening a saved Project this will take you back to the Trimble Connect Window.
- In either case -
- Pick the Project Icon.

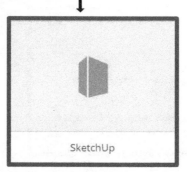

- **Click** on the **Add Folder** option.

- This produces the New Folder edit box

- Backspace and Create a New File – My Warehouse.

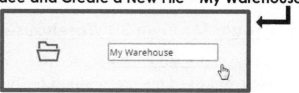

- Click

- Down the **right-hand side of the graphics screen** is the **Details Panel.**
- Pick the **Open button.**
- You are still in the **Trimble Connect Panel** showing a message - **This folder is empty.**
- **You now have a folder in which you can put your 3D models from the 3D Warehouse.**

- **Close SketchUP and then restart.**
- **In the Home Window, Pick the, Create New, tab**
- Pick the **Simple Template - Millimeters** option.
- After a few seconds you have the new untitled model screen view.
- **Go and set the** usual **environment** for a **New Model - units and viewpoint.**
- **Open** the **Components Panel** select the **Search 3D Warehouse** and then enter the name of whatever you are looking for, say a **single bed.**
- From the results - drag the selected model into your drawing area.

- **Pick Untitled** - enter the **name of the model** and click on the **Save Here** button Notice it is saved in the **My Warehouse** Folder.

Trimble Connect

Projects > SketchUp > **My Warehouse**

To put objects from your current model into your 3D Warehouse.
- **Open** the model that contains the object - **Project 1 Bedroom Layout.skp.**
- Select the object – say the **chair.** The blue select box surrounds the chair.

- Press the **Right button on the mouse and click on the copy icon.**

- Click the **File icon** in the **Home Bar.**
- **Select the New option.**
- **In the New Model Graphic Screen**, set the environment - units and viewpoint.
- Press the **Right** button on the mouse and **click on the Paste** icon.

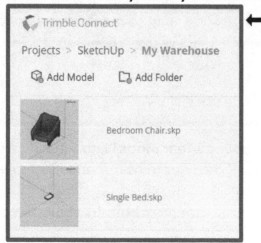

- **The model of the chair is pasted into the new drawing area**
- Pick **Untitled** from the **Home Bar.**
- **In the Name edit box at the bottom of the Connect Panel -** type the name Bedroom Chair and pick Save Here.
- The **Bedroom Chair is added** to the models in **Your 3D Warehouse.**

Bedroom Chair Added to your My Warehouse Folder.

- To get back to the Bedroom model - Pick **SketchUp**

- From the models displayed **select the Project 1 - Bedroom Layout.**

Practice

- Using the methods described, put into the **My Warehouse** the other pieces of **bedroom furniture.**
- **Repeat** for the **Door Frame, Paneled Door, and Window Frame.** We will see how to put **Glass into the window frames in Part 2**
- **Remember** to include sizes -
Door Frame - 2150 x 1000 x 150mm.

Applying Materials

When applying materials, being able to make layers invisible is a great help. The furniture, for example, gets in the way when applying internal colours to the walls and/or applying carpets and tiles to the floor. Being able to remove them makes the task a lot easier. Remember when applying materials, the bounding box must be visible for you to apply the material to individual faces. Applying Tiles to the bedroom floor.

- At the moment if we apply a tile material it will be applied to the entire floor area, both inside and outside.
- We want to restrict the tiles to the bedroom only, the outside of the floor, the apron, to a concrete material.

- **Start** in a **Top Viewpoint**
- Turn **all** the **layers OFF** except - **Layer 0, Walls and the Apron Floor.**
- **Using the line tool and the inside of the walls as a guide, trace the internal shape of the bedroom.**
- Change the viewpoint to **Front-Right Iso.**
- The profile is sitting at the Top of the walls

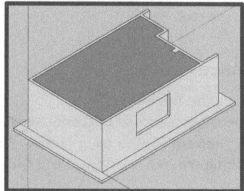

- **Push/Pull - UP 3mm**
- **Make into a group**
- Produce a Layer - **Bedroom Floor Tiles.**
- Using **Entity Info** put onto the **Bedroom Floor Tiles layer**
- **Move the floor pro-**
  file down 2850mm. Make sure you pick the bottom corner of the profile as shown on page 143.

Bottom Corner of the Floor

Endpoint

- Turn the **Wall Layer Off**

- Open the **Material Library** and from the **Tile option** pick a **tile pattern** then apply it to the bedroom floor.

Tiles Applied to the bedroom Floor ⌐

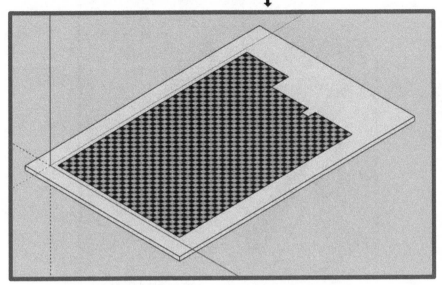

- Apply **a concrete material** to the **apron floor**

- Produce a **carpet area in a similar way to that used on the bedroom floor** and **then apply a carpet material.**

- Apply **materials** to **the internal and external walls.**

- An example of what your bedroom may look like is shown on page 144.

The Axes have been turned OFF and the view is Perspective

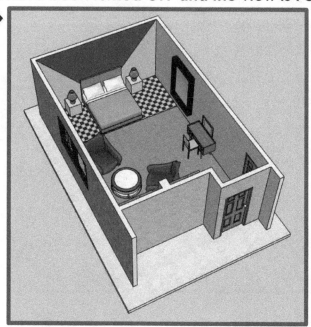

View from Another Angle

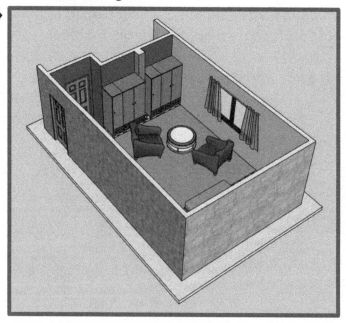

Project 2 – Family Room Layout

Project Details
In this project, you will produce a family room that incorporates the tools and tech-niques used when producing the Bedroom. The only information given is –
- The **shape** of the room **is of your design** but must **cover an area of approximately – 64square metres.**
- The room **MUST** include a **glass sliding door** which leads to a Patio area (not required in your model)
- Has a **minimum of 2 Doors**
- Has a **Minimum of two sets of windows.**
- The **furniture must include –**
  - o **TV**
  - o **TV table**
  - o **Coffee Table**
  - o **Three/four piece suite**
  - o **Table Lights and tables**
- **The Floor is to be Tiled or carpeted or both.**

Project Solution
- Produce **two or three sketches of possible ideas** for your layouts.
- Then **choose one of your ideas.**
- Make a more **detailed layout** that includes
  - o **Sizes of walls**
  - o **Position of doors and windows**
  - o **Sizes of the doors and windows**
- **Knowing where to position the doors and windows allows you to start to indicate on your plan where to place the furniture.**
- **On completion of your layout sketches produce an Action Plan to be used in producing your Family Room.**

The Basics - Part One

An Example, of what your Family Room may look like is shown -

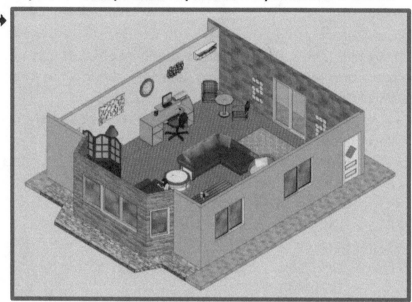

View from Above

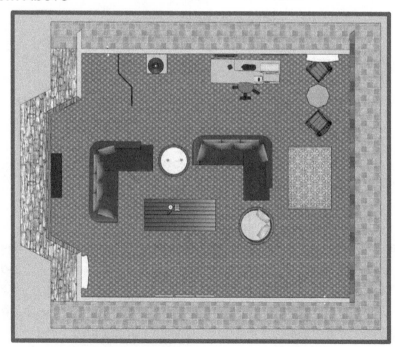

Another Angle

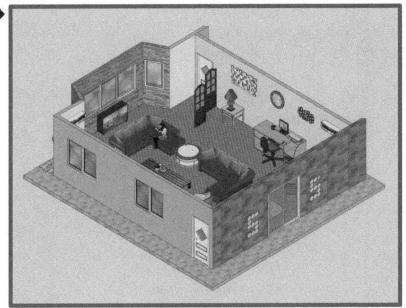

- Remember to put the varying furniture, doors, and windows into your warehouse so you can use them in other projects.

Summary

The aim of Part One has been to introduce you to SketchUp Free. Part One can also be used to guide you through earlier or later versions of SketchUp. By using the basic tools and techniques covered in Part One, it has shown how quickly a 3d model of a mechanical part or architectural building can be constructed. The important tools that need to be practised are:

- o The Drawing Tools –
  - ▪ Rectangle Tool
  - ▪ Line Tool
  - ▪ Circle Tool
  - ▪ Arc Tools
  - ▪ Polygon Tool

The Basics - Part One

- o The Modifying Tools –
    - Move Tool
    - Push/Pull Tool
    - Follow Me Tool
    - Offset Tool
    - Union Tool
- o Measuring Tool –
    - Tape Measure Tool
- o Select and Altering Tools –
    - Select Tool
    - Erase Tool
    - Paint Bucket Tool
- o View Panel Tools –
    - Orbit Tool
    - Zoom Window Tool
    - Zoom Extents Tool
    - Pan Tool

The important techniques that need to be practised are:

- o Use of Layers
- o Creating Groups and Components –
    - Entity Info
- o Use of the Bounding Box
- o Use of the Flip option to Mirror Objects
- o Use of Infer when using the Push/Pull tool
- o How to Import from the 3D Warehouse
- o Creating your own warehouse

The work covered has shown you the very basics of SketchUp Free, and has given you the foundation for the next level - The Basics Part 2. It is now up to you to go and use, develop and enhance what you have learned.

PART 2

HOW DO I

GET STARTED

WITH

SKETCHUP

FREE

MORE ADVANCED METHODS

General Contents of Part Two

Architectural Modelling

The Basics - Part Two

The Basics - Part Two

HOW DO I GET STARTED WITH SKETCHUP FREE
-
MORE ADVANCED MODELLING
METHODS & TECHNIQUES

The How Do I Get Started - Part 2 To Do List

With the Knowledge on how to use Basic Tools and Techniques of SketchUp Free learned from The Basics – Part 1, the next stage is to see how to carry out more advanced methods and techniques into its use including;

- Other uses of the Erase Tool.
- Using Style Pane Browser options.
- Other uses of the Move/Copy to produce multi-copies (arrays).
- Producing layout drawings in SketchUp and getting them ready to be turned into 3D Models.
- Creating Walls, Windows and Doors
- Creating Roofs.
- Applying Materials
- Importing objects from the Warehouse
- Realistic Views

Mechanical Models
SketchUp is generally known for its use in the architectural/interior design field, but it can also be used to produce mechanical models. To see how to use some of the advanced methods mentioned you can; **Produce an assembled 3D Model of the - Heavy Duty Hinge Parts shown.**

Start with an **Action Plan** – this will give some guidance as to how to produce the model

Heavy Duty Hinge Parts Drawing

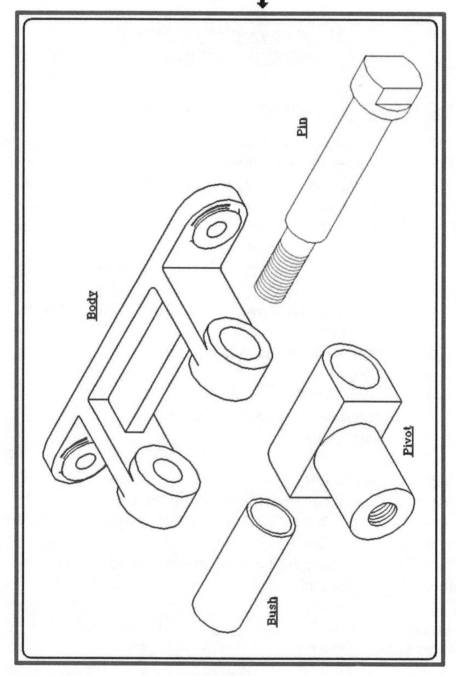

How Do I Produce An Assembly of the Heavy Duty Hinge

Action Plan

- Produce the Body using the Body 2D drawing.
- Using the 2D drawings, produce the Bush and Pivot – use the Array and the Follow Me Tool to produce the internal screw threads.
- Using the 2D drawing, produce the Pin – use the Follow Me and Array to produce the external screw threads.
- Put each object on to its own separate layer.
- Apply the materials.
- Assemble the parts.

Hinge Body 2D Drawing ⌐

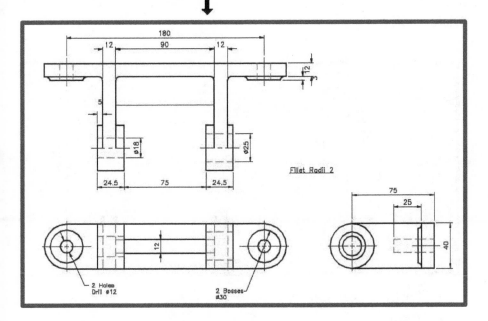

- **Start SketchUp Free**

- Use the - **Simple Template – Millimeters.**

- **Set the Units** and Produce a **Parallel Projection and Top View.**

- **Leave the Views Panel displayed** to save having to go to the Panels Bar each time you need to change views.

- **Save the Model as – Heavy Duty Hinge.**

- **Use the dimensions shown in the Plan View** as a guide - **produce the profile of the Hinge Body.**

- Start by **producing the basic profile** with the **aid of Guidelines** as shown –

Basic Profile

- **Push/Pull up 40mm.**
- Then -
  - o Use the **circle tool** to produce the **end radius's.**

The Basics - Part Two

- Use the **Push/Pull tool** to produce the **arcs and basic shape**

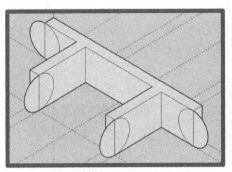 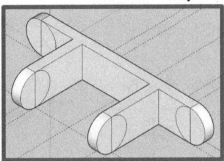

- **Delete the guidelines.**
- **Erase** the edge **line** that **divides the two circles** on the two arms -

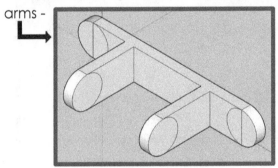

  o On the **Right Arm – Push/Pull 5mm.**
  o On the **Left Arm – Push/Pull 7.5mm.**

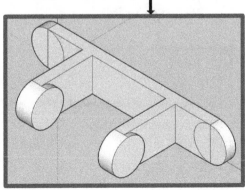

  o **Orbit to reveal the left faces of the arms.**
  o **On the Right and Left Arms – Draw a 40mm dia' circle.**

The Basics - Part Two

o **Erase the edge line** that divides the two circles on the two arms -
o On the **Left Arm – Push/Pull 5mm.**
o On the **Right Arm – Push/Pull 7.5mm.**

View After Push/Pull

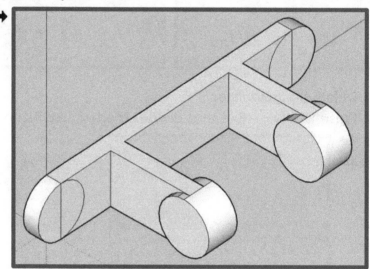

- You now need to put in **the 18mm dia' and 25mm dia holes** in the **two arms.**
  o **Using the Circle tool Produce the 18mm dia and the 25mm dia circles.**

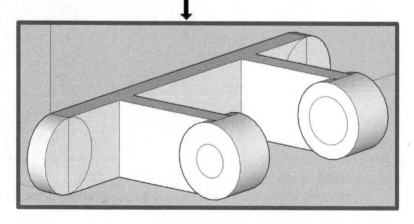

o **Push/Pull to produce the holes.**

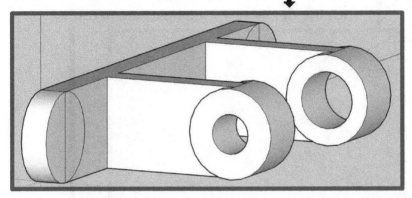

o **Using the same technique on the back face, produce the two 30mm dia' x 3mm bosses with the two 12mm dia' holes.**

o Produce a **Front-Right Iso viewpoint** as shown

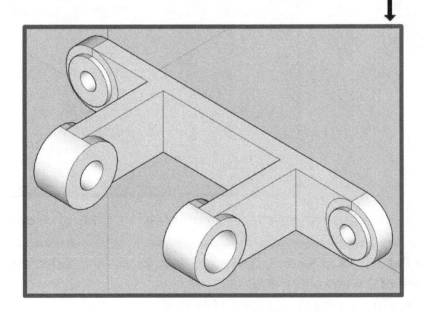

- **You need to check that the Push/Pull tool produced the 12mm dia holes all the way through to the back face.**
  - o Pick the **Back-Right icon** from the **Views panel.**

- If your model is similar to the one shown –
  - **Pick the select tool, then pick the shaded parts and press the delete key – the holes are revealed.**

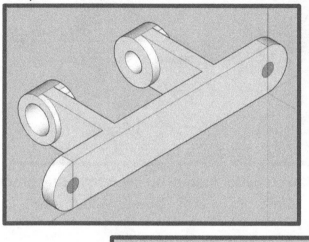

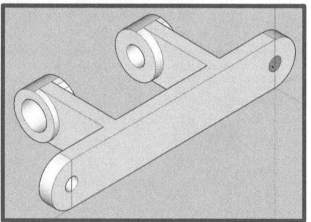

- **Next,** change the current view to a **Right-Front Iso.**

For the model to take on a more realistic look you need to **remove some of the unwanted lines.**

- To do this you use the **ERASE Tool.**
- Selecting the Erase tool and then selecting a line will erase the line but if the line is part of a boundary edge then the surface will be erased.

- **Check this out** – pick the **Erase Tool** and then select **the line indicated** –

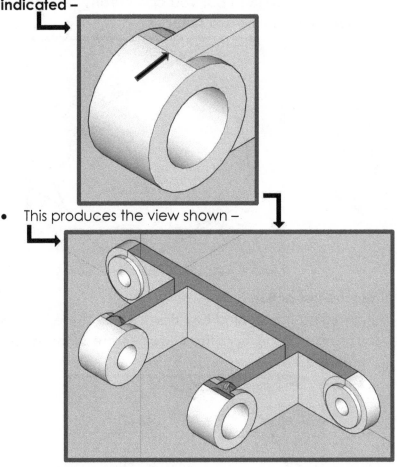

- This produces the view shown –

- **Clearly not what is wanted.**

- **To achieve the result wanted you can use two other methods that involve the use of the Erase Tool** –
    - o Holding the **Shift Key** down and selecting a line will **Hide** the line.
    - o Holding the **Control Key** down will **Soften** and **Smooth** the edge.
- **To check this out - undo the last action.**

- Holding the **Shift Key down** – select the same line.
    - o The line is **hidden** but you can **clearly see the difference between the two surfaces –**

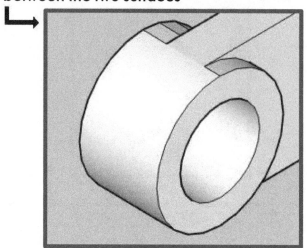

- **Undo the last action**
    - o Holding the **Control Key down** – select the same line.
    - o Using this method **the surfaces are smoothed and blended.**

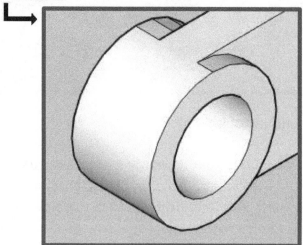

One of the problems in hiding or softening **is getting to see the lines to hide or soften.**

- **A technique often used is by using one of the options found in the Style Panel in the Panel Bar.**
- Pick the **Style Panel** - this produces the **Home Style Pane.**

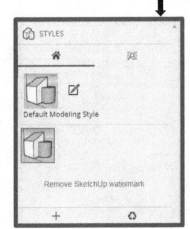

- Now pick the **Browser icon.**

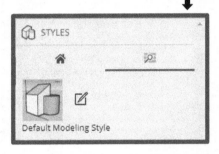

- This now shows the **different styles that can be used.**

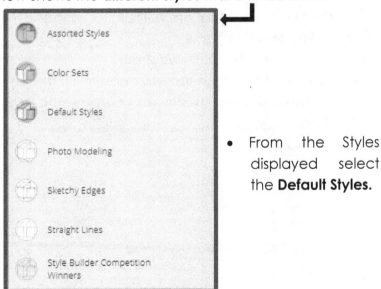

- From the Styles displayed select the **Default Styles.**

- **Select one of the options to see the effect it has on the model.**
- Have a look and **see what happens when you use the other options.**

The Default Style Options

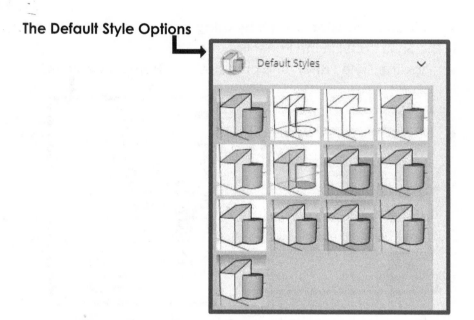

- **The two options that are suitable** for us to see the lines - **are the X-Ray and Wireframe.**
- Go back and select – **Wireframe.**
- The use of the Erase tool will depend on the view you have. If you have a view as shown, you have no lines that need removing.

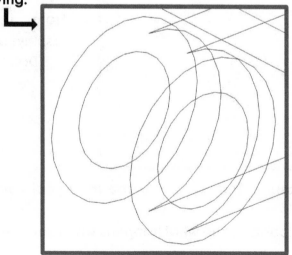

- **But, if you have a view as shown -**

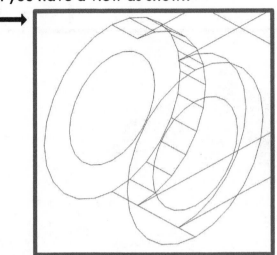

- **Using the Control Key and Erase Tool – remove the unwanted lines.**

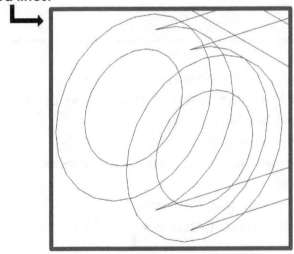

- **Using the method shown - Remove the lines of the other arm.**
- **Check the – Shaded With Textures**
- Also, **soften the edges on the back wall** and don't forget to **repeat for the bottom of the Hinge Body.**
- On completion use the **Shaded with Textures style.**

View using the Shaded With Textures Style

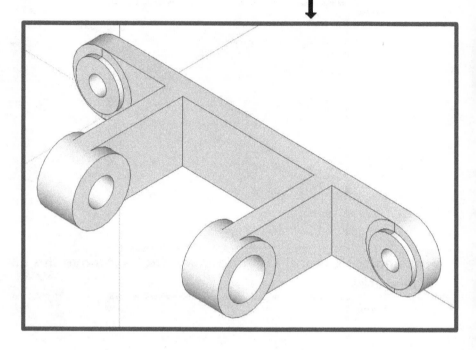

- To complete the model you need to –
    - o Put the 2mm fillets in the corner of the arms and around the 30mm boss.
- Create the Strengthening web.
- For the 2mm Fillets in the corners of the arms -
    - o Go to a TOP viewpoint.
    - o Create the four 2mm arcs.
    - o If you get the message

app.sketchup.com says

Number of segments is too large for given angle and radius.

OK

- Pick the **OK** button - **this undoes the arc drawn - re-position the arc tool** where the **centre point of the arc is to go.**

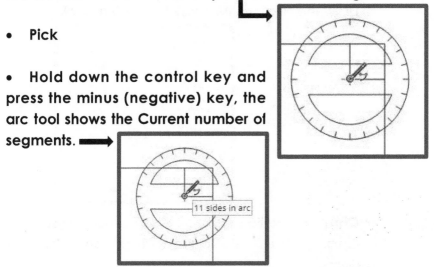

- **Pick**

- **Hold down the control key and press the minus (negative) key, the arc tool shows the Current number of segments.**

- **Keep holding down the control key and press the minus key - the number of segments is reduced.**
- **Reduce the number to 6.**
- **Draw the 2mm arc.**
- **Orbit** and then **use the Follow Me tool** to create the fillets.
- **Soften the Fillet lines** using the Control Key and the Erase tool method.

Fillet lines Softened

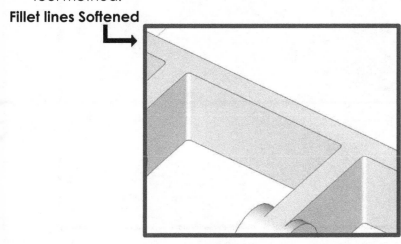

- For the **2mm Fillet for the 30mm dia' boss** –
  - o Pick the **Right view icon.**
  - o **Draw the Fillet profile away from the model.**

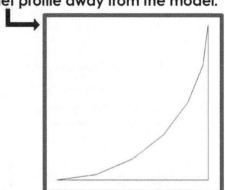

  - o **Copy the profile** for the other 30mm dia boss.
  - o Change the View to **Front-Right Iso** – then **Zoom Extents.**
  - o **Move profiles into position.**

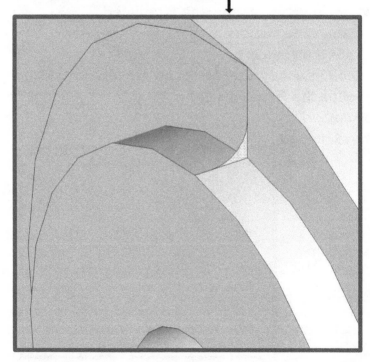

- You now need a circle for the Follow Me path.
  - **Using the Select tool pick the edges of the 40mm dia' circle** as shown –

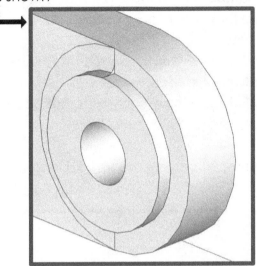

  - **Using the Follow Me tool produce the Fillet.**
  - **Repeat for the other arm.**
  - **Remove the unwanted arc and lines.**

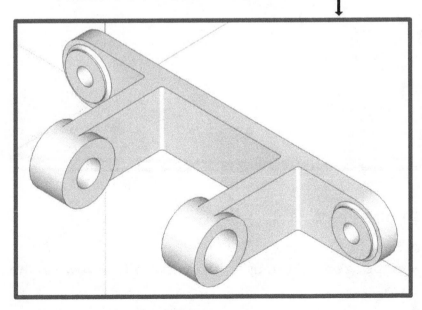

- You now need to create a strengthening web.
- Draw the **90mm x 25mm x 12mm web away from the model** and **remember to put the 2mm radius in the two back corners.**
- **Group then Move into position.**
- You now need to –
    - o Create a **Component** of the Hinge Body **called Body.**
    - o **Create a Body Layer.**
    - o **Put the Hinge Body onto the Body layer through** the use of the **Entity Info** option.

- On completion your model will be the same as that shown.

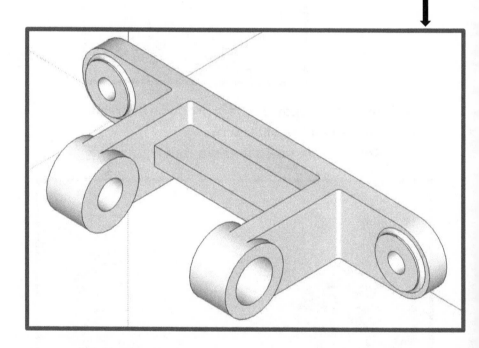

Bush and Pivot

Pivot Bush

- Produce the Bush using the information shown in the 2D drawing

Pivot Bush 2D Drawing

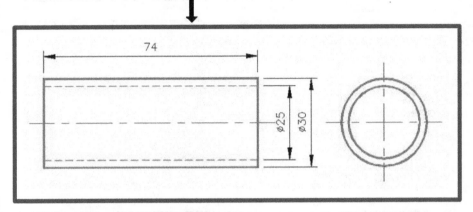

- Turn the **Body layer Off** and then produce the **Bush.**
- Create a **Bush layer** and using – Entity Info - put onto the Bush layer.
- Make the **Bush a Component.**
- Your Bush will look Like -

Completed Bush

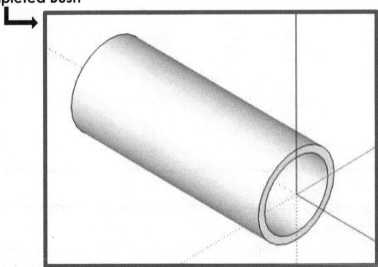

- **Make the Body layer visible** so you can see where it is in relation to the Bush.
- **Move the Bush down say - 150mm**

Bush Moved Down

- **Turn both layers Off.**

Pivot 2D Drawing

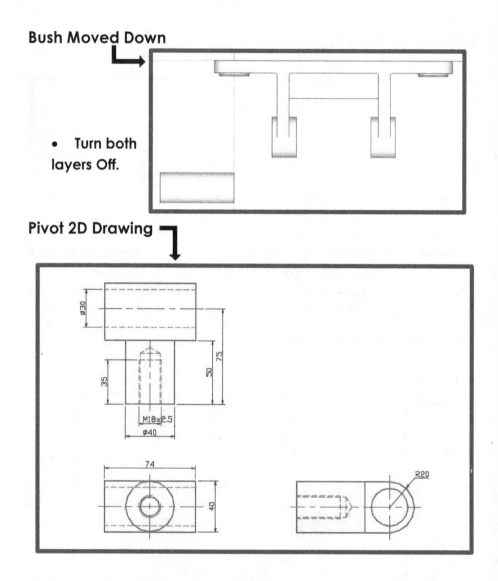

It can be seen from the drawing that the pivot has an internal screw thread. You will find that a large number of mechanical parts have screw threads so it is important that you know how to go about being able to produce a **representation of both internal and external threads. A representation of a screw thread will be good enough as the majority of models do not require a true helix thread.**

Before proceeding in the production of screw threads it would be a good idea to have an understanding of some of the terminology used

Screw Threads

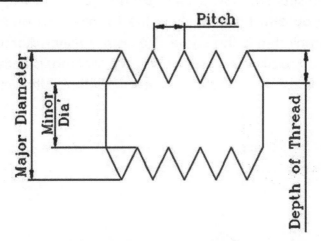

Pitch = The Distance from one thread to the same position on the next thread.

Depth of Thread (DoT) = Major Dia' – Minor Dia'

Major Diameter = Outside diameter (OD)

Minor Diameter = OD – 2xDoT

Depth of thread is estimated for drawing purposes and in general, is drawn **1mm smaller each side when the Major Diameter is less than 15mm.**

When the Major Diameter is **between 16mm – 25mm the DoT = 1.5mm each side.**

When the Major Diameter is **between 26mm – 35mm DoT = 2mm each side.**

The major diameter and the pitch should always be given e.g. M8x1.25

M = metric; **8** = major diameter; **1.25** = the pitch

In most instances, the thread produced does not have to be an exact representation of a real screw thread but a very close simulation.

When constructing threads that do not go all the way through the object, you also have to show the tapping drill profile. A taping drill is a drill that is the same size as the Minor diameter and the hole produced is used as a guide to a tool that is known as a TAP. The tapping tool cuts the metal to produces the internal screw threads.

A profile for this type of internal screw thread would be similar to that shown –

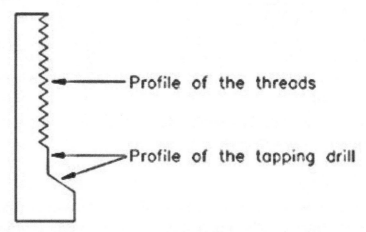

The distances of the Tapping drill profile are ¼ of the Major Diameter from the last screw thread plus another ¼ for the drill point.

Example

For an M20 diameter thread the tapping drill profile distances would be 5 + 5.

Before commencing on the construction of the pivot, have another look at the information given on screw threads.

How Do I Produce the Pivot Thread Profile

- **Zoom in on the Axis Origins**
- Thread required is an **M18 x 2.5mm pitch.**
- Depth of Thread = **1.5mm**
- The profile of the internal thread will look the same as that shown.

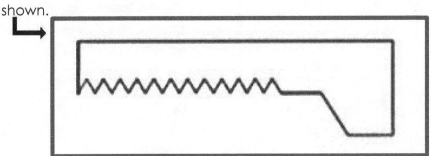

- Start with a **construction box** using guidelines the **distance up from the axis equal to the Minor Dia** in this case **7.5mm** and **Major Dia = 9.0mm.**
- From the **vertical axis** use a guideline **2.5mm (the pitch).**

- Using the **Line Tool** draw the shape of the **screw thread.**

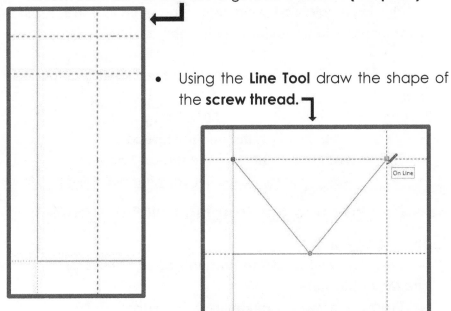

- **Erase the guidelines and the horizontal line used to find the midpoint.**
- To produce **the Array –**
    - o **Copy the two lines** that form the screw thread – **Pick**

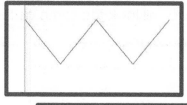

- o In the **Distance edit box type - 13x** and then **press the Enter key.**

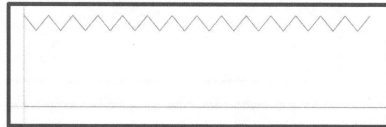

- **This has produced multi-copies (12 + 1) of the screw thread.**
- Why **13x**
- **This is calculated by – dividing the pitch into the depth the threads have to travel into the tapping drill hole.** For the **M18 x 2.5mm –**

Depth of thread travel = **35mm (see the drawing of the Pivot).**
Pitch = **2.5mm**
Number of threads required = **35/2.5 = 14**

- Array = **14 minus(-) 1, the original thread.**
- This gives a total of **13 (12 + the thread copied).**
- You now need to produce the **Tapping drill Point Profile.**

How Do I Produce the Tapping Drill Point Profile

Tapping Drill Point
- **Produce a vertical line from the apex of the last thread on the Minor Diameter.**
- Produce a vertical **guideline 4.5mm from this line.**

The Basics - Part Two

- Produce a second vertical **guideline 9mm from the line**
- Using the Line tool – **draw the tapping drill form**

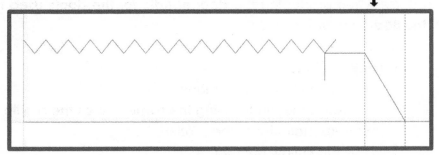

- **Erase the unwanted lines.** ➡️

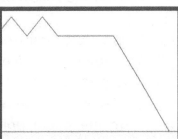

Profile

- **To produce the completed profile**
- Using the **Line Tool**
  - From the endpoint of the left screw thread (Green axis) draw a line that goes Up 11mm
  - Draw a second line 50mm to the right - (you get the message – On Red Axis)
  - Draw a third line down 20mm (On Green Axis)
  - Close the line on the point of the tapping drill form –

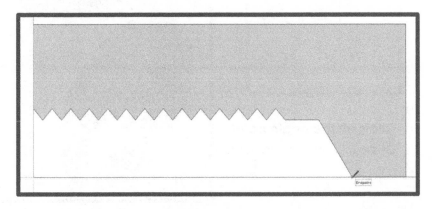

Producing the Pivot Arm

- **The method used is the same** as that used in Part 1 of the course **when producing the door handle for the doors used in the Bedroom Project.**

- **A quick reminder -**
    - o Produce the **profile – (done)**
    - o Produce the **circle using the same axis as the profile but perpendicular to the profile**
    - o Use the **Follow Me tool**

- Change to a **Front-Left Iso** viewpoint
    - o **Move the profile 20mm to the right along the Red axis** to give room for the circle.
    - o Select the **Circle tool and move so that the centre is on the origin point** the circle lies **parallel to the top viewpoint.**
    - o **Press** the **Right Direction Arrow** to produce a **Left Viewpoint** ⌐

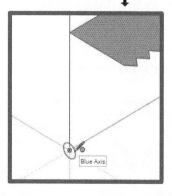
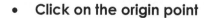

- **Click on the origin point**
- **Draw the 30mm dia' circle**

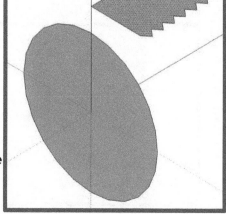

- **Click the Circle**
- **Select the Follow Me tool.**
- **Click on the profile** - if the profile does not revolve - follow the profile of the circle.
- **Erase the circle**
- This produces a view as shown.

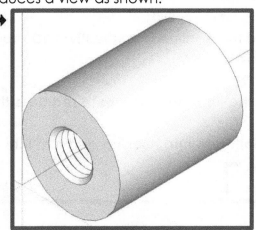

- **Make the Pivot Arm a Group.**
- Create a **Pivot layer**
- Using the **Entity Info put the Pivot Arm onto the Pivot Layer**
- To check the internal screw thread –
- **Go to a Top Viewpoint and put the X-Ray mode ON.**

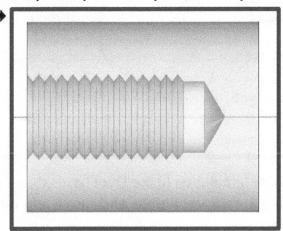

To complete the Pivot - produce the part that holds the bush.

Bush Housing
- **Turn the X-Ray Off by selecting the - Shaded with Textures option.**
- **Move** the Pivot Arm **70mm to the left.**
- Turn the **Pivot Layer OFF.**
- **Using the Information from the Pivot 2D drawing produce the Bush Housing.**
- Turn the **Pivot Layer ON**
- **Position the housing and arm to produce the completed Pivot part.**
- Select **both arm and housing** and **turn into a component named Pivot.**

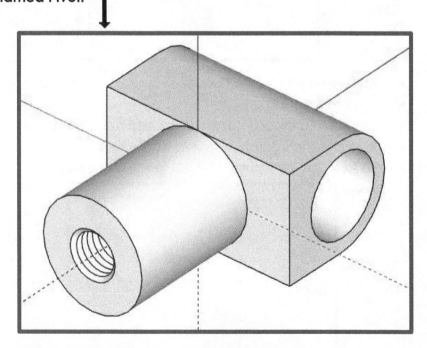

- **Using Entity Info put on to the Pivot Layer**
- **Make the Bush layer visible and move into position in the pivot housing.**

Applying Materials

- Using the **Materials library** apply a material or colour to both the Bush and Pivot.

Colours Applied from the Materials Library

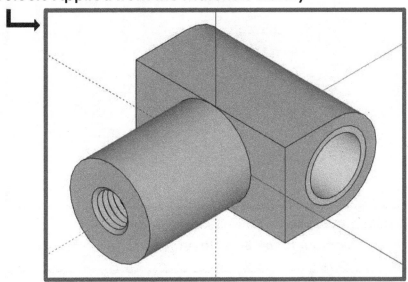

Positioning the Body, Pivot and Bush
- Make the Body Layer visible.
- Move the Body so that the holes in the two arms are in line with the holes in the Pivot and Bush.

X-Ray View From the Right Side ⌐

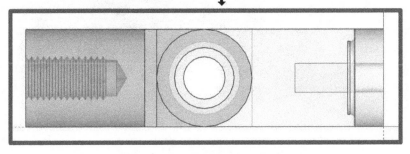

The Basics - Part Two

- **An X-Ray view will show you if you are in alignment** ⌐

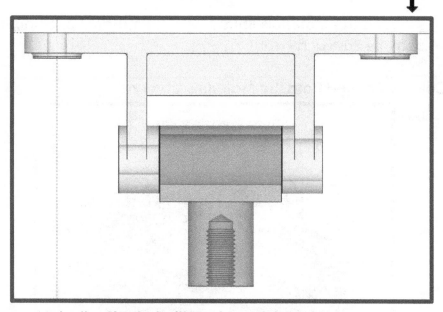

- Make the **Shaded with Textures style current.**
- **Apply a colour to the Body layer.** ⌐

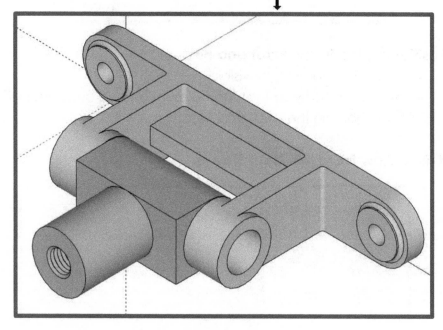

Completing the Model

The Pin
- **Produce a 3D model of the Pin**, using the **information** shown in the 2D Drawing.

2D Drawing

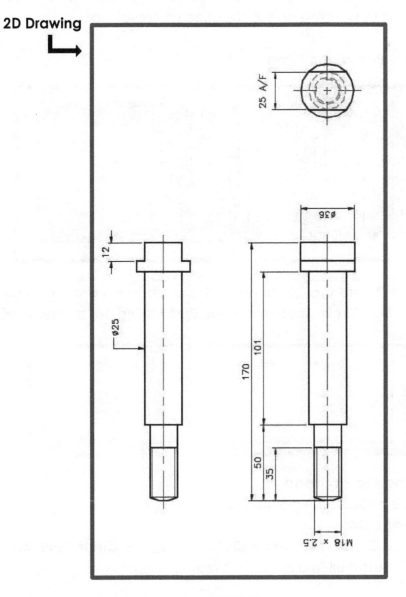

- Make the **Body, Pivot and Bush invisible.** Create a **Pin layer.**
- **Using the techniques shown on screw construction produce an External M18 x 2.5mm pitch screw thread, with a DoT of 1.5mm.**
- On completion, the threaded 50mm part of the Pin should be the same as that shown - yours may have a different shading depending on the direction you revolved.

Threaded Part of the Pin⌐

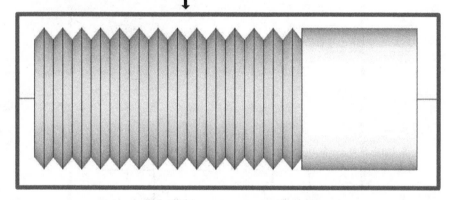

- The **25mm dia' shoulder** of the pin can be **produced by using the Circle Tool and then Push/Pulled to a length of 101mm**

Producing the Pin Head
- The head of the Pin is produced in Two Stages –
- **Stage One –**
    - ○ **Create the 36mm dia' by using the Circle Tool, and Push/Pull to a length of 19mm.**

- **Stage Two –**
  - **Producing the 25mm Across Flats (A/F)** is produced by creating two rectangular columns.
  - **The columns when placed in position, when deleted, will produce the edges of the intersection which are push/pulled to create the 25mm flats.**

Stage 1

- **Produce the 36mm dia' by 19mm long Pin Head.**
- But **Don't Group** at this stage.

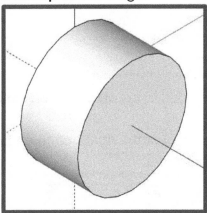

Stage 2

- **To produce the 25mm A/F,**
- **you need to produce two rectangular columns that are bigger than the required 12mm x 5.5mm.**
- **Produce two columns** that are **15mm x 10mm** with a **height of 40mm.**
- **Make each column a Group.**
- **Produce guidelines 12 x 5.5.**
- **Using the guidelines, position the columns – Use the X-Ray**
- **style to help** position the columns.

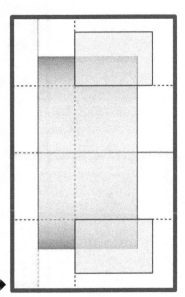

- **Make sure the columns protrude as shown** -

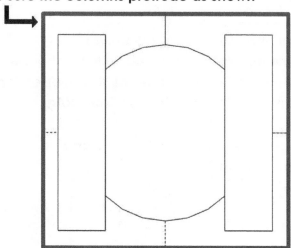

- The **columns** are used to **create the intersection lines** on the **Pin Head.**
- **Pick a column** then **pick the right button on the mouse** - this brings up the **context menu.**

- Select the - Intersect Faces and the option - With Model

- Repeat for the other column.
- Erase the Two Columns and guidelines

You have shown the intersecting lines of the two columns.

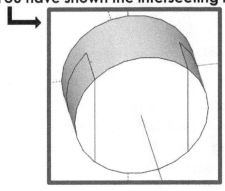

- Use the Push/Pull tool to create the 25mm Across Flats (A/F)

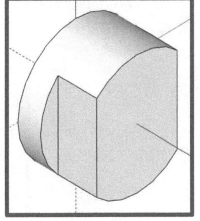

- The final task for the Pin Head is to make it a Group
  - Make the Pin Head a Group
  - Using Entity Info put onto the Pin Layer.

With all the sections that go to make up the Pin completed the next thing to do is put them together.

- Arrange the sections as shown

- **Then carefully move them so that the left face of the shoulder and head are touching the right face of the threaded section and shoulder.**

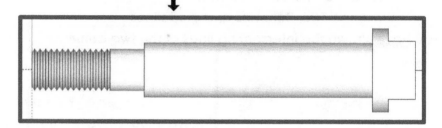

- **If you need to find the distance to move –**
  - **Use the Measuring tool - pick a point on the Shoulder and the corresponding point on the Pin Head,** for example, the distance between is the distance that has to be moved.

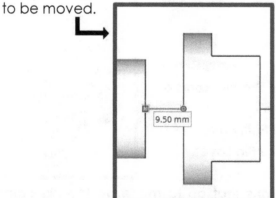

- **The Pin will look like that shown**

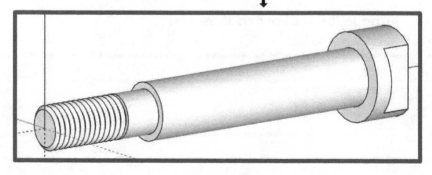

Making the Pin a Solid Model

- To make the Pin a single solid model, the Union option from the Outer Shell Group of Tools has to be used.
    - o **To Union** pin sections - **Go to the Outer Shell Tool select the Union Tool option.**
    - o **Click on** the **threaded end**, the **shoulder and head** - the **three parts are joined together to form a solid.**

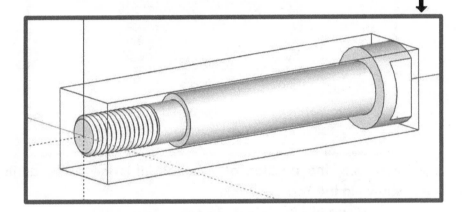

- Using the Entity Info put the pin onto the pin layer.
- Apply a colour to the Pin.

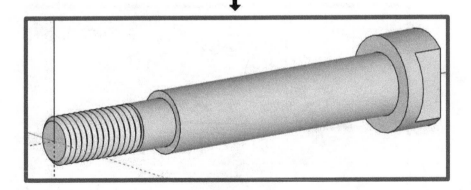

- The pin now has to be positioned but first –
    - o **Make the Body, Bush and Pivot Visible**
    - o **Go to a Top viewpoint**

Top Viewpoint

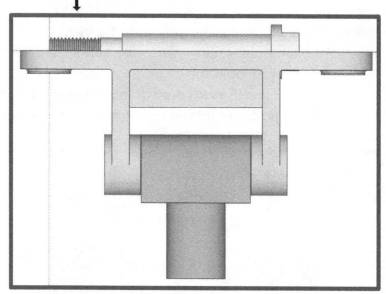

- Assuming the position of your model is the same as that shown in the Top Viewpoint -
    - o Move the Pin DOWN 75mm
    - o Then move to the RIGHT 13mm leaving a 2mm gap between the Right Arm of the Body and the Pin Head.

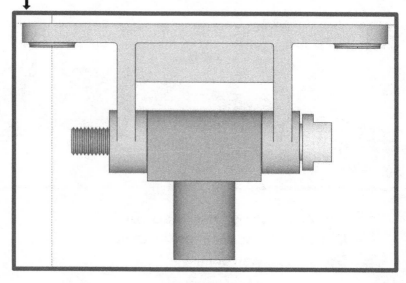

- **Check to see that the Pin is centred in the Bush and Body Arm Holes** by **selecting the Left viewpoint.**

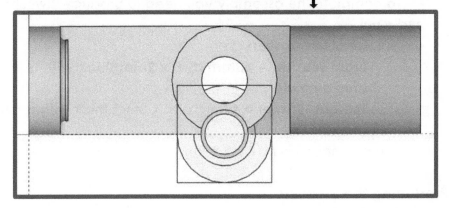

- As can be seen, in this case, **the pin has to be moved up 20mm.**

- Once you have the pin in position the model will be similar to that shown.

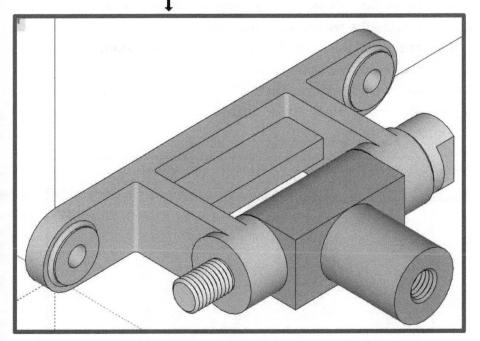

How Do I Complete the Hinge Bracket

- To complete the assembly you need to produce 2 washers and a nut.
- The **size of the washers** are –
  - o **Right Washer = 40mm dia' x 2mm thick with a hole 26mm diameter**
  - o **The Left Washer = 40mm dia' x 3mm thick with a hole 19mm diameter.**
- You also need an **M18 x 2.5 Nut.**

Producing the Washers
- **Go to a Right viewpoint**
- **Find the centre of the Pin Head** and **draw a circle, 40mm dia.**
- Make the **part layers invisible.**
- **Copy the circle 50mm to the Right**
- **Draw the circles for the holes** – 26mm dia and 13mm dia.
- **Create the two holes in the washers.**
- **Push/ Pull** the 40mm dia circles **2mm and 3mm**
- **Make each washer a Group.**
- **Using Entity Info put onto a Washer layer.**
- **Make the body Layer visible and move the two washers into position.**

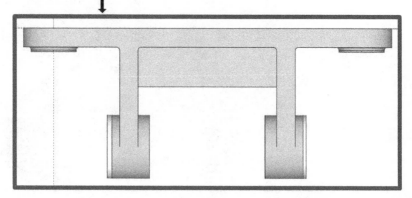

Producing the Nut

- The nut to be produced is similar to the Head of the Pin but with the following sizes–
    - **Outside Diameter = 40mm**
    - **Length = 21mm**
    - **A/F = 25mm**
    - **Depth of Flats = 15mm**
    - **Thread = M18 x 2.5**
    - **DoT = 1.5mm**

- **The construction method is similar to that used for the internal thread of the Pivot.**
- **Do the construction along the Red and Blue axes starting at the origin point.**
- To calculate the Number of threads –
    - **21/2.5 = 8.4**
    - **Ignore the 0.4 so -**
    - **The array will be 8 – 1 = 7**
- **Layout the guidelines to construct the thread and profile.**

Guideline Layout

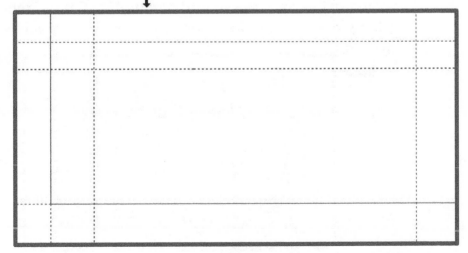

- **Draw the thread and copy.**
- **Array 7x.**

- This leaves the thread short of the 21mm guide line.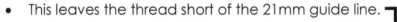

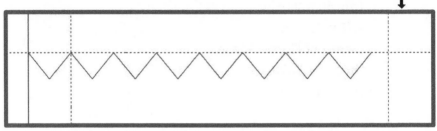

- **Copy a Right Flank (slope) line** and put it **in position on the end thread** ⌐

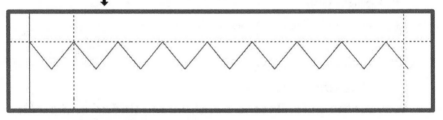

- **The overhang can be removed on producing the profile.**
- **Produce the profile using the line tool –**
    - ○ Start at the left screw thread and go 11mm up, 21mm along, and down to the intersection on the right screw thread.

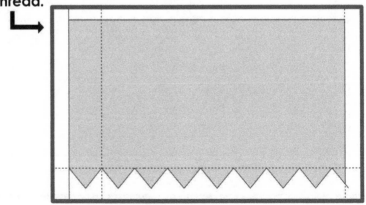

- **Erase the overhang and remove the guidelines.**

- Pick the **Front-Left Iso.**

- Draw a 10mm dia circle from the axes origin intersections

  o Move the circle 40mm Right, along the Red Axis.

  o Select the Follow Me tool and then pick the screw profile.

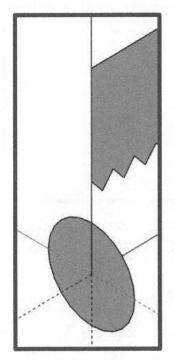
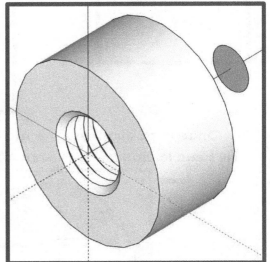

- **Erase the Circle.**

- **Using the methods shown for the Pin Head, produce the 25mm flats using rectangles of 20mm x 15mm x 40mm.**

- **Make each rectangle a Group.**

- **Use Guidelines to help position the rectangles,** you might have to **use the X-Ray option to see the guidelines.**

The Basics - Part Two

Using the X-Ray to See the Guidelines.

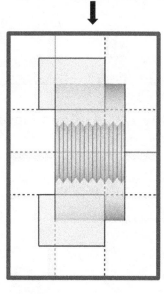

- Check to see if the rectangles have to be moved up 20mm.

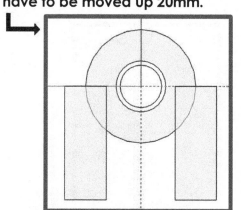

- Once in position, use the method shown to produce the Pin Head to produce the 25mm A/F.

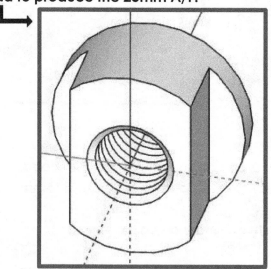

- Make the Nut a Group

- **Apply a Colour to the Nut.**
- **Create a Nut layer and using Entity Info put onto the Nut Layer**
- Make the following layers visible – **Bush, Washers and Pin.**
- Go to a **TOP Viewpoint.**
- **Move the Nut 75mm down and then 13.5mm to the Right.**
- **Check to see if the nut is centred by going to a Left Viewpoint.**
- **Move so the nut is centred** if you have to.

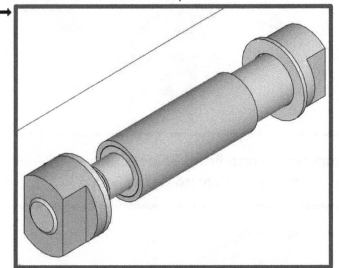

- Turn the **Axes Off** by selecting the **Display Panel** and **Clicking the Axes Check box -**

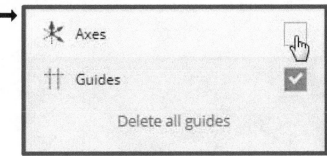

- **Make the Body and Pivot layers visible.**

- Go to a **TOP Viewpoint**

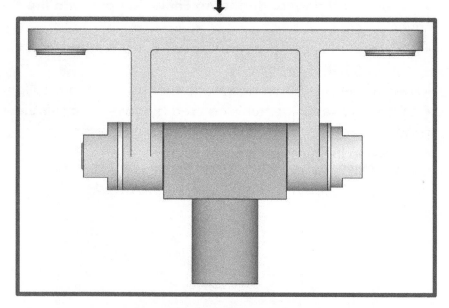

The Completed Hinge Bracket looks like -

- Select the **Front-Right Iso** viewpoint

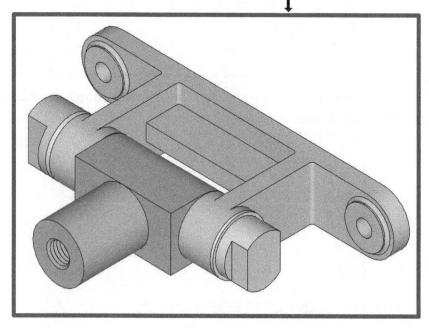

- The Hinge Bracket from a **Left-Right Iso** Viewpoint

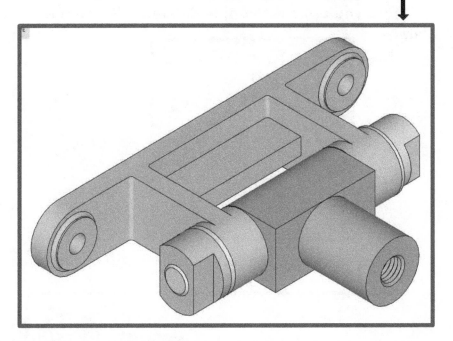

Before moving on it will be a good idea to take a look at the new commands and techniques used.

Erase Tool -

- Selecting the Erase tool and then selecting a line will erase the line but if the line is part of a boundary edge then the surface will be erased.

Erase Tool Hide Method

- Selecting the Erase Tool and holding the **Shift Key** down and selecting a line will **Hide** the line.

Erase Tool Soften and Smooth Method

- Selecting the Erase Tool and Holding the **Control Key** down will **Soften** and **Smooth** the edge and make it blend with the surface.

Styles –

- Gives you options to apply different effects, a few are shown –

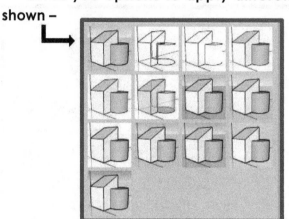

- Shaded With Textures ⌐

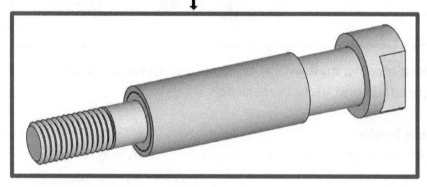

- Default Style ⌐

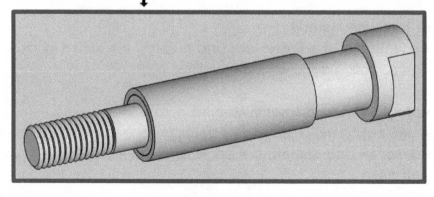

- **X-Ray Mode**

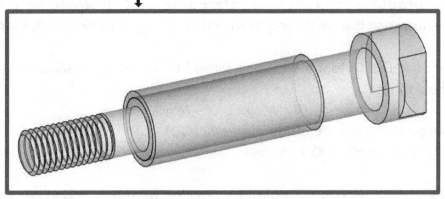

- The X-Ray options can be **used to expose lines that are hidden from view.**

- **Simple Style**

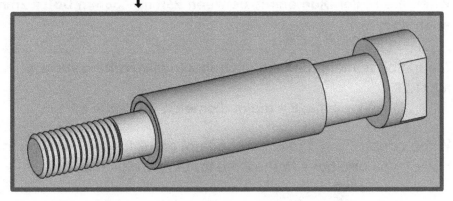

Fillets –
Used to give strength where objects meet at right angles.
- Produce the fillet shape using the **Line and Radius Tools.**
- **Put into position and use –**
  - o **The Push/Pull Tool for Linear fillets**
  - o **The Follow Me and Circle Tool for Circular fillets.**

Screw Threads –

To produce Internal and External threads it would help to remember the basic requirements that need to be produced -

Pitch = **The Distance from one thread to the same position on the next thread.**

Depth of Thread (DoT) = **Major Dia' – Minor Dia'**

Major Diameter = **Outside diameter (OD)**

Minor Diameter = **OD – 2xDoT**

Depth of thread is estimated for drawing purposes and in general is drawn 1mm smaller each side when the Major Diameter is less than 15mm.

When the Major Diameter is between 16mm – 25mm the DoT = 1.5mm each side.

When the Major Diameter is between 26mm – 35mm DoT = 2mm each side.

The major diameter and the pitch should always be given e.g. M8x1.25

> **M = metric; 8 = major diameter; 1.25 = the pitch**

When constructing threads that **do not go all the way through** the object, **you also have to show the tapping drill profile.**

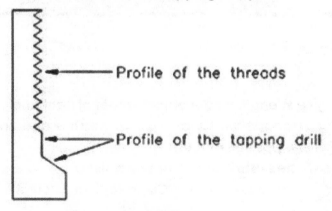

Profile of the threads

Profile of the tapping drill

The Basics - Part Two

The distances of the Tapping drill profile are ¼ of the Major Diameter from the last screw thread plus another ¼ for the drill point.

ARRAYS
Used when multi copies of an object are required both in a circular and linear pattern. The Radial tool is used for circular arrays and the Move tool for linear arrays. **For screw threads a Linear array is required.**

Linear Array –
- **To calculate the number of threads required –**
  - **Dividing the pitch into the depth or distance the threads have to travel.**

- **To Produce the screw thread profile based on the Major diameter, Pitch and Depth of Thread.**
  - **Move/Copy the profile of the first thread drawn.**

- **Array by entering -**
  - **The Number of threads (n) – 1(the original thread) followed by a multiply symbol.**
  - **n-1x**
  - **Example if n = 8; array = 8-1 = 7x**

Thread Profile –
- **Complete the profile.**

- **Produce a circle perpendicular to the profile.**

- **Use the Follow Me tool and select the profile or select the profile and then follow the red circular path of the circle to complete the internal or external thread.**

Solids –

Provided the shape has a volume and is completely closed in all directions and is either a Group or a Component a solid will be created.

Union –

- To Union - **Go to the Outer Shell Icon in the Toolbar**, from the **group of tools displayed** select the **Union Tool**.
   - o **Make sure each object to be joined together is touching or over-lapping.**
   - o **Using the Union Tool select each object to be joined together** to create the solid.

Subtract –

- **Create the object to be subtracted from - but don't at this stage make it a Group.**
- **Create the object to be subtracted - make it a Group.**
   - o **Position the object to be subtracted on the object it is to be subtracted from.**
   - o **Select the object to be subtracted – bring up the context menu - select the Intersect Faces - With Model.**
   - o **Erase the object to be subtracted which reveals the intersecting edges.**
   - o **Use the Push/Pull tool to remove the shape created by the intersecting edges.**
   - o **Make the finished object a group or component.**

Project 1

Bearing Press Assembly

Using the 2 Dimensional drawings of the various parts of a Bearing Press -

2D Drawing - Bearing Press

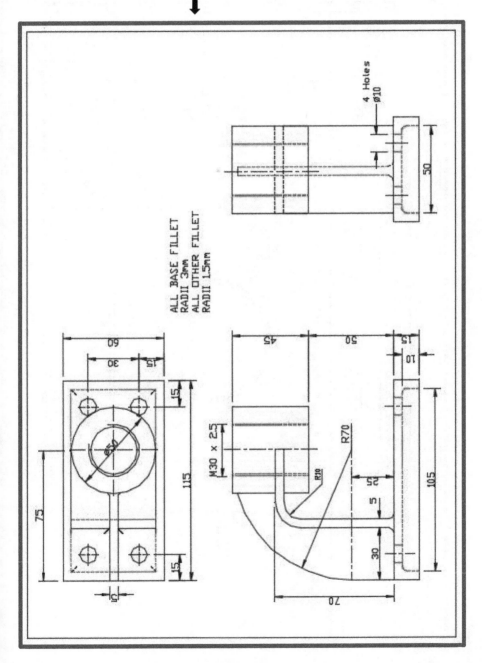

2D Drawing - Bearing Press Parts

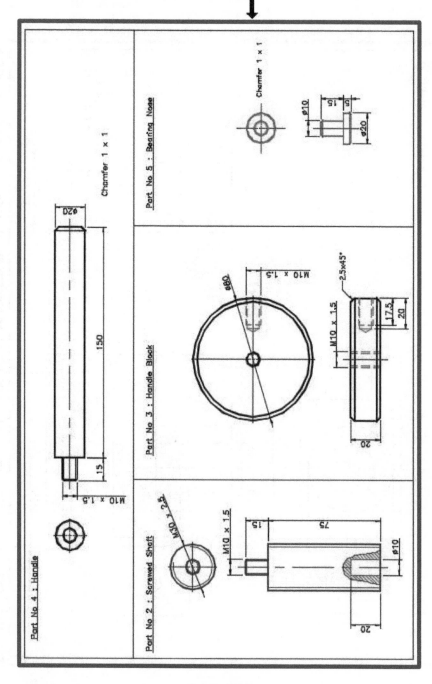

The Basics - Part Two

2D Assembly Drawing – Bearing Press

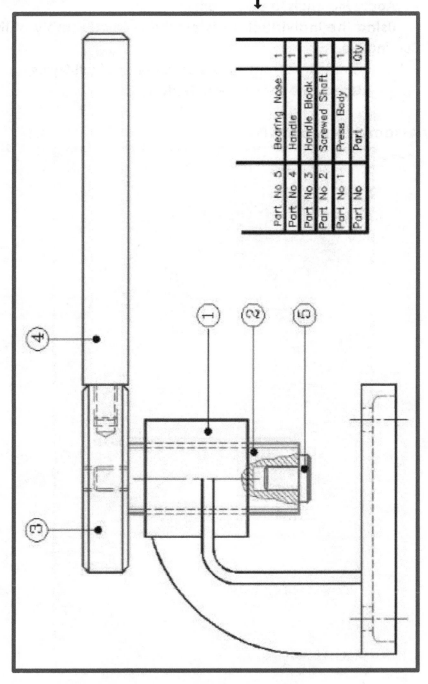

Part No 5	Bearing Nose	1
Part No 4	Handle	1
Part No 3	Handle Block	1
Part No 2	Screwed Shaft	1
Part No 1	Press Body	1
Part No	Part	Qty

- **Produce individual 3D Models of each part.**
- **Apply Materials to each part.**
- **Using the individual parts produce an Assembly of the Bearing Press.**
- On completion; **From the Styles Panel – Default Styles**
  - **Check the Shaded With Texture.**
  -

3D Assembly – Bearing Press

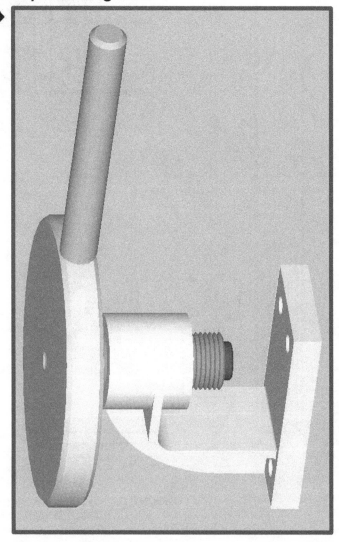

Architectural Layout and 3D Models

Producing 3D Models From Layout Drawings Using

SketchUp Free

SketchUp is used more for producing architectural/interior models than mechanical models. 3D models of buildings are constructed from the Layout drawing (Plans). Layout drawings can be either imported into SketchUp or drawn in SketchUp. In SketchUp Free you are restricted to certain types of file for insertion. As we are going to use the layout of the bungalow shown, we will do the layout in SketchUp. On completing the layout you can produce the 3D Model of the Bungalow, design the colour scheme of the interior and insert the various pieces of furniture.

How Do I Produce a Layout Drawing in SketchUp

Layout Drawing of the Bungalow - Project 1

- If just **a very basic model** is required the layout **would show the walls only.**

- If a **more detailed model** is required then **the walls and the** positions of the doors and windows would be shown.

- In **our SketchUp model,** we are **going to show the position** of the walls, doors and windows.

Floor Plan

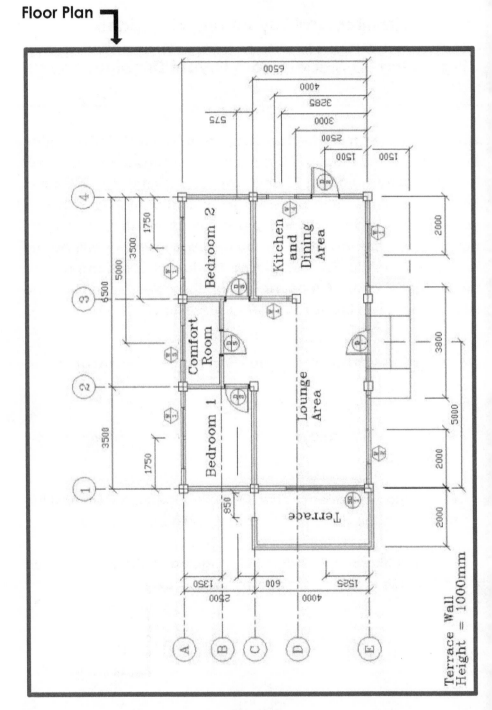

Terrace Wall Height = 1000mm

Door and Window Details

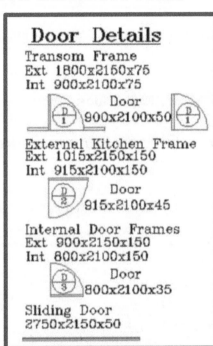

Door Details

Transom Frame
Ext 1800x2150x75
Int 900x2100x75

Door
900x2100x50

External Kitchen Frame
Ext 1015x2150x150
Int 915x2100x150

Door
915x2100x45

Internal Door Frames
Ext 900x2150x150
Int 800x2100x150

Door
800x2100x35

Sliding Door
2750x2150x50

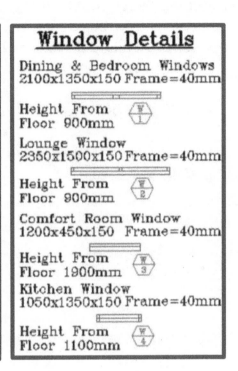

Window Details

Dining & Bedroom Windows
2100x1350x150 Frame=40mm

Height From
Floor 900mm

Lounge Window
2350x1500x150 Frame=40mm

Height From
Floor 900mm

Comfort Room Window
1200x450x150 Frame=40mm

Height From
Floor 1900mm

Kitchen Window
1050x1350x150 Frame=40mm

Height From
Floor 1100mm

Furniture Layout

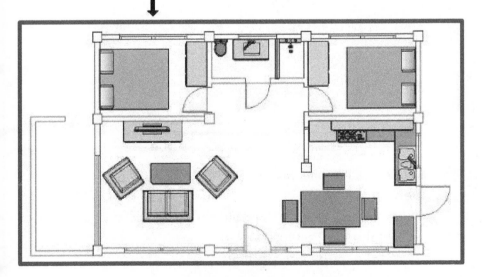

The Basics - Part Two

Producing the Layout Drawing

- **Start SketchUp and set the Drawing Environment. Use a Style of Shaded with Textures.**

- **Using the drawing shown on page 212 produce the layout.**
  - •

- **Start** with the **measuring tape tool to layout the centre position of the walls.**

- Use the **Line tool to put in the centre line of the walls.**

- **Delete the varying areas.**
- **Then -**
  - o **Produce a 300x300 column** using the rectangle tool.
  - o **Make the column a group.**
  - o Move/copy into position.

The Basics - Part Two

Columns Placed in Position

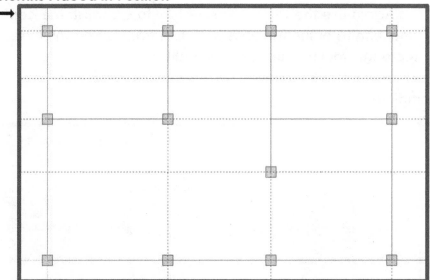

- Use the measuring tape tool to layout the walls and the Terrace walls.
- Use the rectangle tool to put in the walls.
- Put in the Terrace wall using the Line tool.
- Remove the Guidelines.

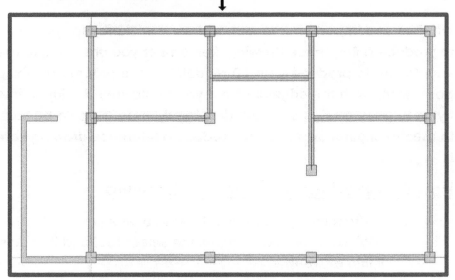

- **The next step is to position the windows and door frames.**
- Again **use the tape measure tool to establish the centres and lengths of the windows and door frames** and then **use the rectangle tool to produce their profiles.**
- Your completed layout will look similar to this –

Completed Layout⌐

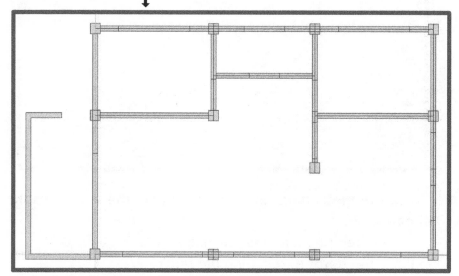

- Save the Layout as **- BUNGALOW - PROJECT 1**
-

Whether you import your layout or draw it in SketchUp, you need to produce a Reference Drawing. Remember you are going to use your layout to produce your 3D Model. If in the process anything goes wrong with the original layout you could spend a lot of time trying to put the original layout drawing right. So it would be safer to use the original drawing and produce a reference drawing from it.

How Do I Produce A Reference Drawing

- **Start with making the layout drawing a Group -**
  - o Window the drawing **with the Select Tool** and then **turn it into a Group –**

Grouped Layout

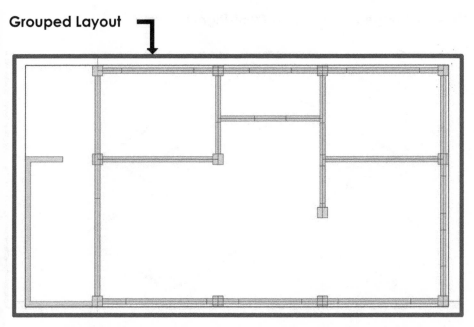

- **Check the alignment of the drawing** with the Red and Green axes. **You really only need to do that if you import a drawing.** As you used the axes to produce the layout you know that the walls align.

- At the moment the centre point of the column is on the origin point. **Move the drawing so that the bottom left corner of the bottom left column is on the origin point of the axis.**

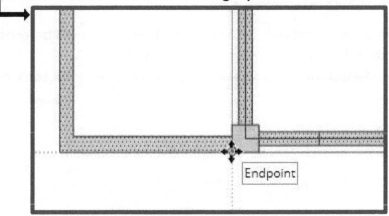

- **Change the view to a Front-Right Iso**

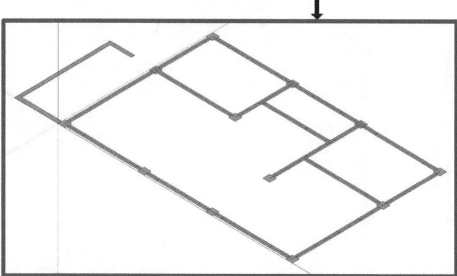

- **Create a NEW Layer named - Layout**

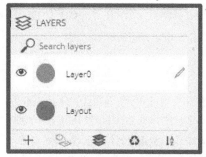

- **Put the grouped Layout onto the Layout Layer using Entity Info.**
- **Just to make sure;** Turn the **Layout** layer **Off - the drawing disappears** – and **On.**

- At the moment the **Reference layer could still be erased or moved, so to make sure we can't do either –**
- **Select the drawing – Right click and select the Lock option.**

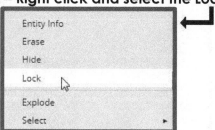

- The Grouped lines change colour to signify they are locked

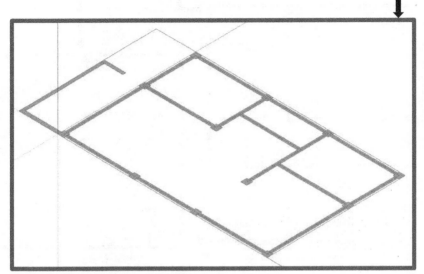

- Try and **erase or move** the layout drawing – **nothing happ-ens.**
- **Pick a point outside the layout using the select tool - the red lines disappear.**
- Try and **erase or move** the layout drawing – **nothing happ-ens.**
- **Even though the red lines do not show your layout is still locked**
- **Before you can start to model, you have one more thing to do –**
  - o **Make it easier to switch the Reference layout On and Off.**

How Do I Turn the Reference Layout On and Off

When working on your 3D model you find that the **reference layout can get in the way during construction.** It would be more convenient to be able to quickly switch it on and off. To do this you use the **Layers and Scenes options**. The Scenes option is found in the Views Panel.

The Basics - Part Two

- **From the Panels Bar open the Layers and Views options –**

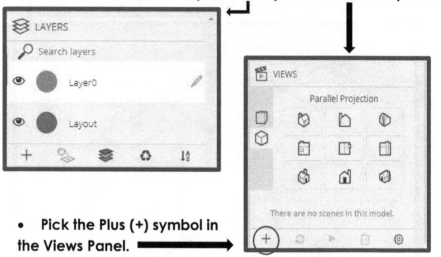

- **Pick the Plus (+) symbol in the Views Panel.**

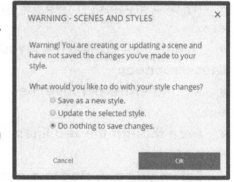

- **If you get - WARNING - SCENES AND STYLES**
  - **○ Pick - Do nothing to save changes.**

  - **○ Pick the OK button**

- This produces the current view in the scenes window.

- **Pick the Scene 1** and change the name to **Layout ON** then press the **Enter key.**

The Basics - Part Two

Scene 1 Changed to Layout ON

- **Pick the Update Scenes icon.**

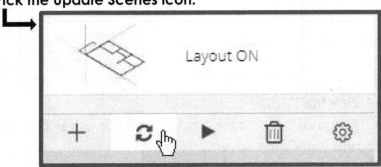

- **This produces the Scene Update details list –**

- **The only option need-
  ed is the –**
- **Visible Layers –**
- so **remove the check
  marks in all the other
  check-boxes.**

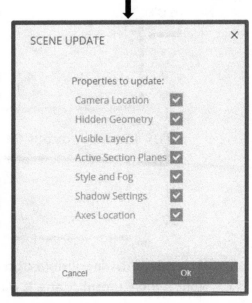

SCENE UPDATE   ✕

Properties to update:

Camera Location ☑
Hidden Geometry ☑
Visible Layers ☑
Active Section Planes ☑
Style and Fog ☑
Shadow Settings ☑
Axes Location ☑

Cancel   Ok

- In the **Layers Panel –**
  remove the check
  mark in the **Layout**
  check- box – the
  drawing disappears.

- **Create the second scene – repeat the process used for the first –**
    - o **Pick the +(plus) icon –**
    - o In the **Name edit box** type – **Layout OFF** – press the **Enter key.**

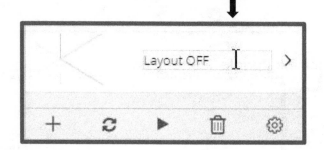

- **Pick the Update Scenes icon.**
- **Remove the check marks in all the other check- boxes except the Visible Layers**

- **Just to check -**
    - o Pick scene – **Layout ON** – the drawing becomes visible

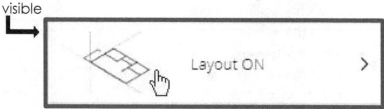

    - o Pick scene – **Layout OFF** – the drawing disappears.

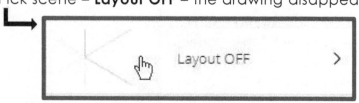

- **Make the drawing visible again.**
- **Notice the Current scene is a uniform colour**

The Current Scene is a uniform colour

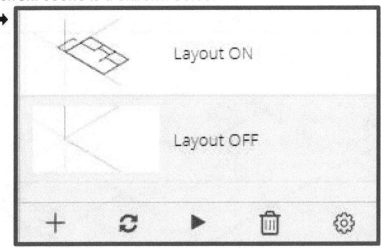

This completes the preparation of the Layout drawing. The methods shown are ones that should be followed each time you need to create a Reference drawing. With practice, the preparation will only take a few minutes.

You now need to go back and practice what has been shown.

Practice

Layout Drawing

- **Undo back to the point where you created a group of the Layout, (the layout layer will disappear).**
- **Repeat the process of producing the Reference Drawing and to make it easier to switch the Reference layout On and Off.**

- You may find that you have to repeat the process a number of times until you don't need to refer to the notes.

On completion, the reference drawings will look the same as that shown –

Drawing Screen View

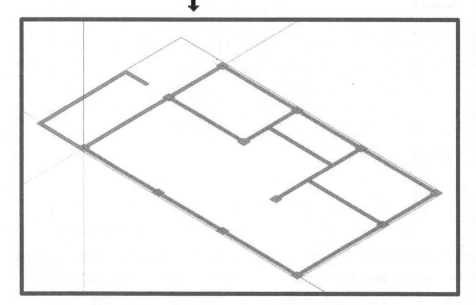

- Save the drawing and then - Exit SketchUp Free

Producing the 3D Model.

What happens next depends on what type of model is required;
- A model that just shows the outline (profile) of the House/ Building in a block form.
- A model that just shows the walls of the House/Building.
- A model that shows the position of the doors and windows by putting in the holes in the walls.
- A model that includes the doors and windows.
- A complete detailed model.

In the 3D model of the Bungalow, the terrace walls can be put in <u>AFTER</u> the Bungalow has been completed.

- Open the Bungalow - Project 1 drawing.

To Remove the Terrace Walls -

- **Select the Layout and right click on the mouse then select the Unlock option.**
    - o **Pick the original layout and right click and select Explode.**
    - o **Create a new layer called - Terrace Walls.**
    - o **Select the Terrace Walls ONLY - make them a group.**
    - o **Use Entity Info and put onto the Terrace Walls Layer.**
    - o **Turn the Terrace Walls Layer Off - this leaves the Main Layout.**
    - o **Make the Layout a Group, use Entity Info and Put onto the Layout Layer.**
    - o **Pick the layout and right click and select Lock.**
    - o **The Grouped Layout lines change colour.**

To show the model as a block –

- The method used **will largely depend on-**
    - o **The size and shape of the house or building.**

- **Two methods can be employed –**
    - o **Use of the Line tool**
    - o **Use of the Rectangle tool**

Line Tool Method

- With this method, you **trace around the periphery of the external walls and columns -**
    - o Select the Line Tool.
    - o **Pick a start point** - say the **bottom right Column.**
    - o **Slowly click on the corner points of the columns and walls** – you get the message – **Endpoint in Group** - at each point.
    - o Use the **Scroll Wheel** to work your way around the periphery.

Using the Line Tool - Choose a Start Point

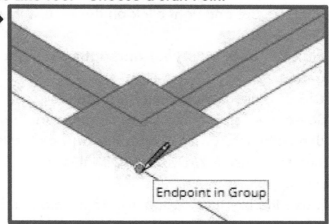

Work Your Way Around the Periphery

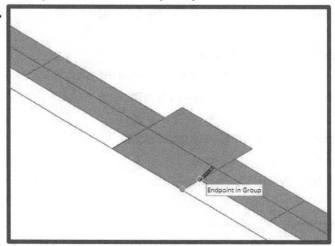

o Keep using the **Line Tool** until you have worked **your way back to where you started.**

o **On picking this last point the area gets filled in.**

- **Turn the reference drawing off** by selecting the **Layout OFF** scene.

- Click on the **Drawing Extents** tool so you can see all of your layout –

Filled Layout Area ⌐

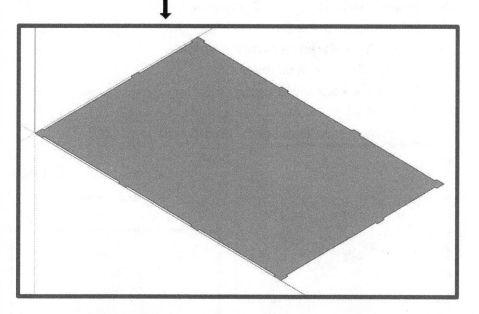

- Use the Push/Pull Tool and pull up 3500mm.
- Click the **Zoom Extents** tool and - from the **Display Panel** – remove the check from the Axes check box.

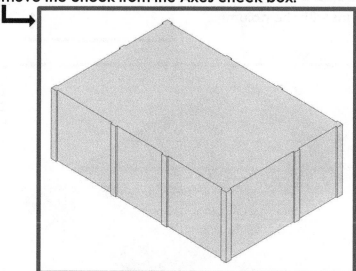

- You have a Block Profile of the Bungalow.

Rectangle Tool Method

- Delete the block of the Bungalow.
- Put the Axes back On.
- Make the Reference drawing visible.
- Turn the Terrace Wall layer Off
- Select the Rectangle Tool.
- Pick a start point -
  o say the **bottom right Column** and

- then the **top left corner**

- This produces a shaded area that overhangs the walls but aligns with the columns.

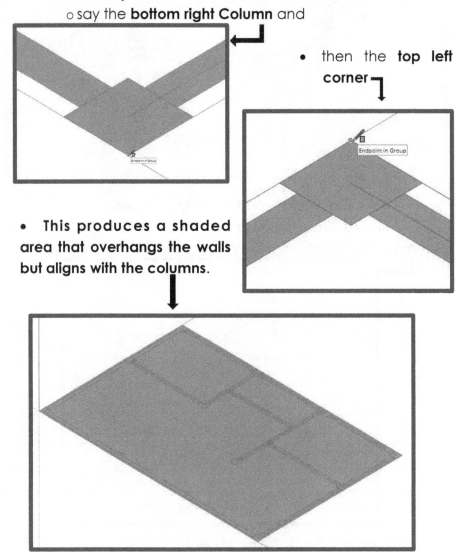

- Use the **Rectangle tool and Erase tool to remove the areas that over-hang the walls** to get a true profile of the bungalow.

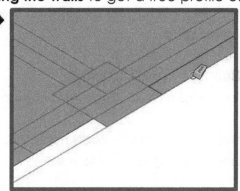

- **Work your way around the Bungalow using the rectangle tool to define the area and the erase tool to erase the defined area.**
- Pick the **Layout OFF scene** to give a clearer view of the defined area.

With the Reference Layout Off, this gives a clear view of the Defined Area.

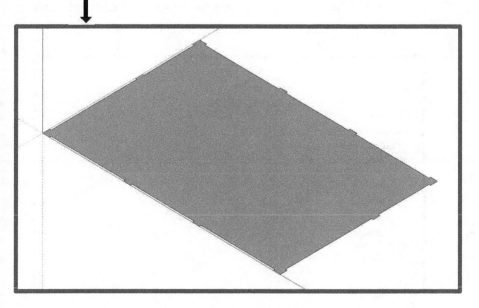

How Do I Show the Model with Walls

- The method used will largely depend on the size and shape of the house or building.
- The methods employed are –
    - The Line tool – small buildings
    - The Rectangle tool – large rectangular shaped buildings
    - A combination of Line, Rectangle, Circle and Arc tools – buildings having varying forms.

For the layout of the Bungalow, because of the columns, a combination of both Line and Rectangular tools will be used.

Combining the Use of the Line and Rectangle Tools
- Delete the block of the bungalow.
- Make the **Reference drawing visible.**
- Repeat the method shown on producing a block profile.
    - **Use either method.**
    - **Pick the Layout OFF scene** to give a clearer view of the defined external bungalow profile.⌐

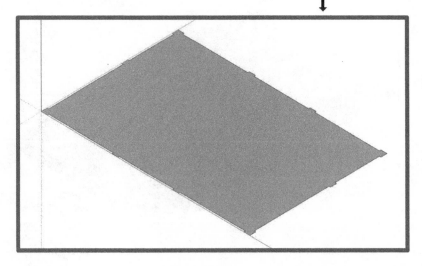

- To define the external walls –
  - o Use the **Offset tool** and **pick a point on the profile between the columns.**

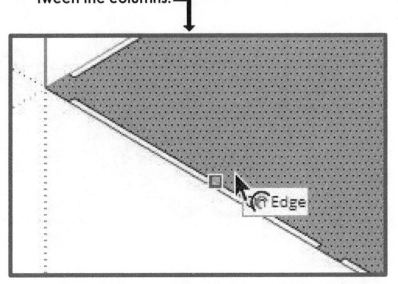

  - o **Enter an Offset distance of 150** then press the **Enter key**
  - o **Delete the inner area,** as this is not required -

Inner Area Deleted

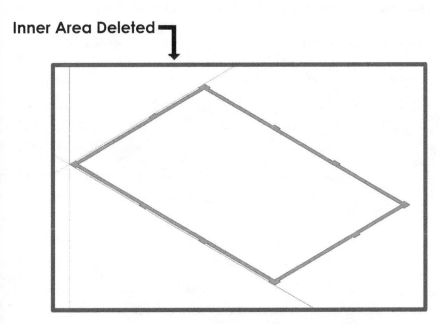

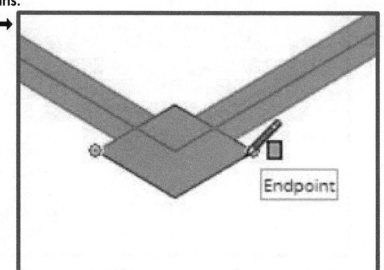

- Pick the **Layout ON scene and pick the layout** to show the **Reference Layout.**
- **Using the Rectangle tool, go round and produce the columns.**

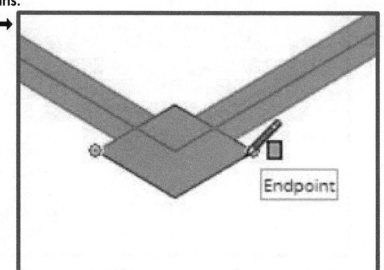

- **Delete the inner area,** to produce the view shown.

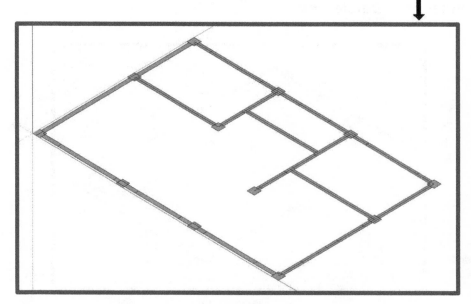

- Erase the unwanted lines within each corner column.

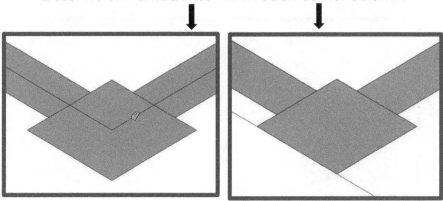

- **You now have to join together the external walls and external columns so that they become one unit.**
  - o To do this, you **erase the lines where the walls and columns meet.**
- Pick the **Layout OFF scene** to remove the Reference layout.

Making the External walls and Columns One Unit

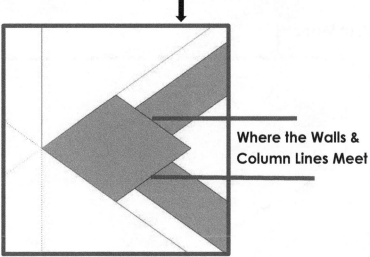

Where the Walls & Column Lines Meet

- Use the **Push/Pull tool** to see if you **have missed any lines** (the walls will not go up if you have).

- Your columns and walls will look like ⌐

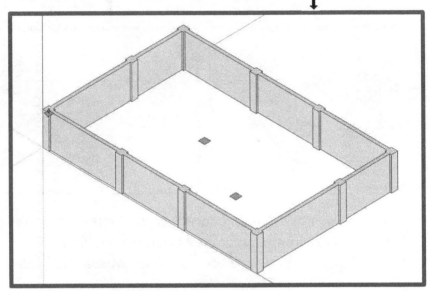

- Once you have your external walls and columns looking as Above, you can put your drawing back in layout mode as shown by pressing the Escape Key.

Layout Mode ⌐

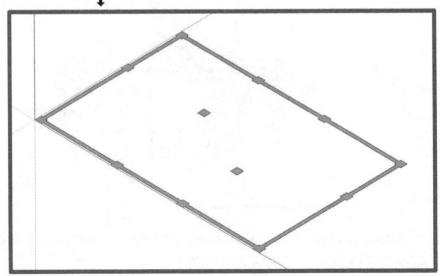

- **On large layouts,** you might want to **create separate groups of the external and internal walls.** This will **separate the internal walls from the external walls.**
- As this layout is not that big, we will group the interior and exterior walls together to form one group.

How Do I Produce the Interior Walls

- **Interior walls are produced in a similar way to the exterior walls by using the Rectangle and Line tools.**
- **Another technique** that can be used in creating both exterior and interior walls, **is by having the layout in a Top viewpoint.**
- **To see how to draw the interior walls in a Top viewpoint –**
    - o Pick the **Layout ON** scene then **pick the layout** to show the **Reference Layout.**
    - o Pick the **Top View** from the Views Panel. ⌐

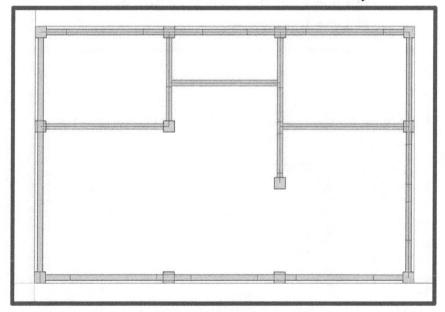

- **The interior walls are shown in red.**
- **Remember to turn the Terrace Wall Layer Off**

The Basics - Part Two

- **Zoom window the Top Left Bedroom area as shown**

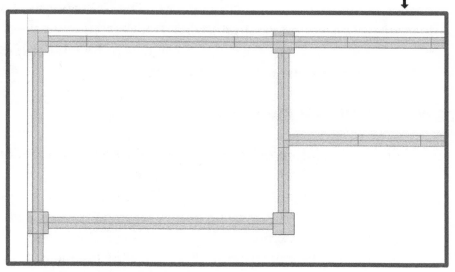

- **Trace over the top of the internal walls** using the Line or Rectangle Tool - **then turn OFF the Reference Layer.**
  - o **This puts back the Front-Right Iso viewpoint.**
  - o **Pick the Top View.**

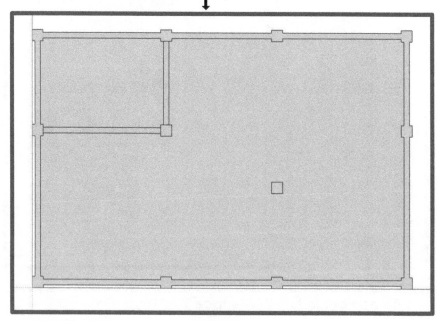

- **Delete** the filled in area.

- **You should get into the habit of turning Off and On the Layout Scenes, so you can see if you are working correctly.**

- **Complete the drawing of the Interior walls** and **on completion pick** the **Layout OFF scene.**
    - o This puts back the **Front-Right Iso viewpoint.**
    - o **Pick the Top View.**

Top View of Bungalow Layout

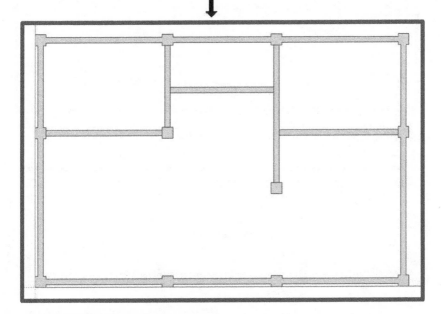

- **As you did earlier -**
    - o **join together the walls and columns.**
    - o To do this - **erase the joining lines.**
    - o The walls and columns become one unit.

- Remember - if you miss a line the walls and columns will not extrude.

The Basics - Part Two

Joining Together the Walls and Columns

- Your completed view will look like this

- To produce the walls –
  - **Pick the Layout ON scene - then select the Layout OFF scene**
  - Using the Push/Pull tool, **extrude the walls to a height of 2850mm.**
  - **Click on the Zoom Extents** tool **and** from the **Display Panel – remove the check marks in the Axes check box.**

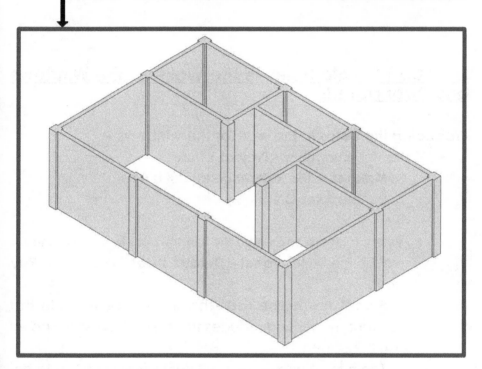

Practice

- You now need to **go back and practice the methods shown** on creating the exterior and interior walls.
- To do this –
  - **Erase the model of the walls**
  - **Pick the Layout ON scene to show the Reference drawing.**

- Using the methods shown produce the Exterior and Interior walls of the house.
    - o Repeat until you can do it without referring to the instruction.
    - o On completion, your model will be the same as that shown on page 239.
    - o Save the model then exit SketchUp.

How Do I Create Holes in the Walls for the Windows and Door Frames

Producing the holes in the wall for the windows –
- Open the **Bungalow - Project 1** model.
    - o **Make sure the Reference layout is ON**
    - o Put the **Axes ON**

- So you can clearly see where the windows are to be positioned.
    - o Pick the **Styles Panel – Default styles** - pick the **X-Ray icon.**
    - o **Select the Home tab -**this shows the styles in the current model and reduces the area of the styles panel on the screen.
    - o **Zoom in** on where the **front right window (W1) is to go, as shown on page 242.**

Referring to the Information given on page 213 on the **window details** the **height from the floor** for Windows **W1 is 900mm** the **external frame size is 2100 x 1350 x 150.**

- Using the **measuring tool and the reference layout** produce the **window W1 guidelines** as shown on page 242.

- Zoom in on the area where the Front Right Window is to go

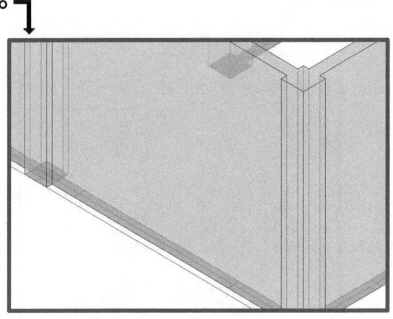

Applying the Guidelines

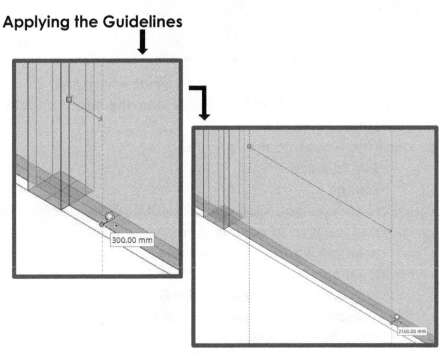

- **Turn the X-ray mode off** and put in the **900mm and 1350mm guidelines**

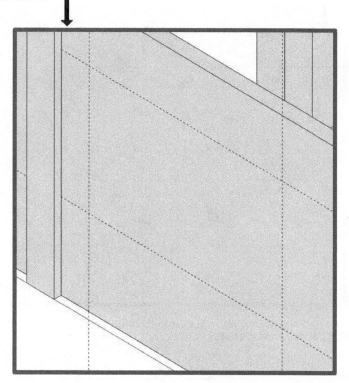

- Use the **rectangle tool** to draw the **window form tool.**
- **Erase the two vertical guidelines and the top horizontal guideline.**
- **Copy the window form tool** to the –
    - o **Two Bedrooms**
    - o **Lounge**
- For the Lounge, you will have to adjust both the height and length of the lounge window form tool.
- For the **length,** you can **use the scale tool**
- For the **height** –
    - o Produce the **1500mm guideline** and then use the **rectangle tool to produce the form tool.**
    - o **Erase the two guidelines**

- With the form tools in there approximate position –

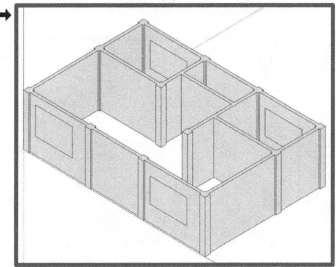

- **You know need to align the copied form tools to the windows in the reference drawing.**
- To do this you use the -
    - **X-ray mode**
    - **Scale Tool**
- **Put the X-ray mode on.**
- **Zoom in on the lounge window.**
- **Select the window form tool.**

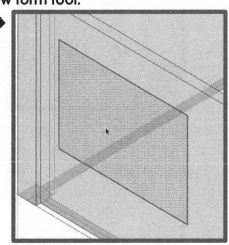

- To adjust the length of the lounge window form tool –
  - Pick the Scale tool

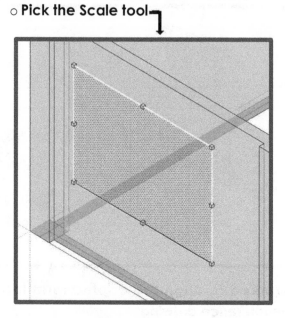

Adjusting the Lounge Window

- Pick the **Left Middle Grab box**
- Drag down onto the corner of the reference window as shown

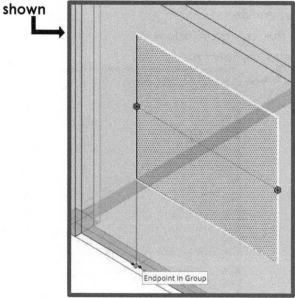

- Pick and Repeat for the other side.
  - The two edges align perfectly with the reference window.

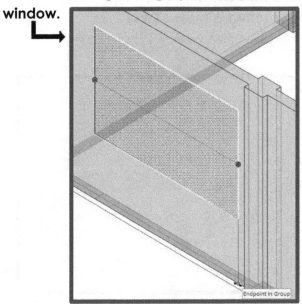

- Repeat the above method for the other three window form tools.
- Using The Push/Pull Tool produce the holes in the walls –

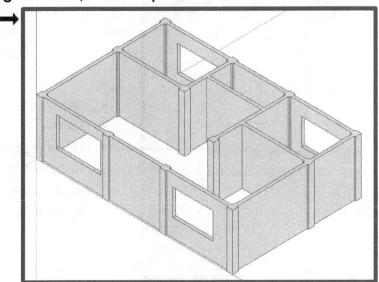

The Basics - Part Two

- You now have to go and **repeat what has been shown** for -
  - The **Bathroom Window (W3).**
  - The **Kitchen Windows (W4)**
- On completion, the walls will look like

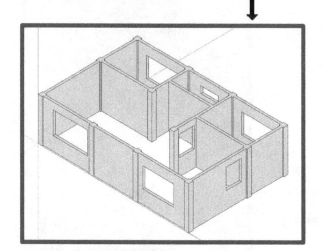

Using the same methods that were used for the windows, repeat for the doors.

- **Zoom in to where the Main door is to go –**

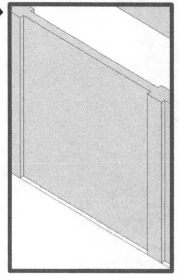

- Using the **Rectangle tool -**
- Draw a rectangle that conforms to the **Transom frame height and width (2150 x 1800) –**

Transom Frame Form Tool Rectangle

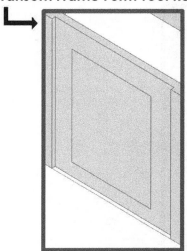 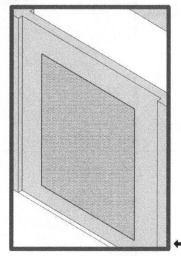

- **Using the Select tool pick the Transom frame Form tool.**
- Now **select X-Ray mode** so you can see where the form tool is to go.
- Using the **Scale tool** adjust the form tool so that it **aligns with the door reference on the Right.**

- **Repeat for the Left side of the door form tool.**

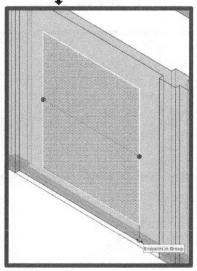

- On completion of scaling use the **Move tool to put the form tool onto the ground –**

Form Tool Moved Down Onto the Ground

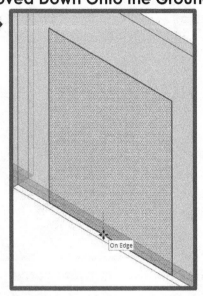

- Use the **Push/Pull** tool to produce the hole in the wall.
  - o Turn **X-Ray mode OFF**

Transom Door Wall Cavity

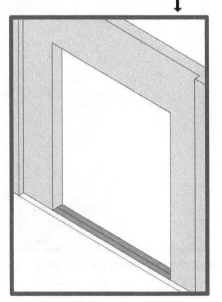

- **Produce the other door frame form tools in a similar way.**

- Remove the Vertical Line displayed on the column in the opening for the Sliding Door.

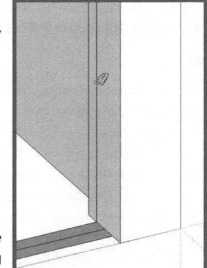

- The walls will be the same as that shown after producing the door frame cavities.

View of the Window and Door Frame Cavities in the Walls

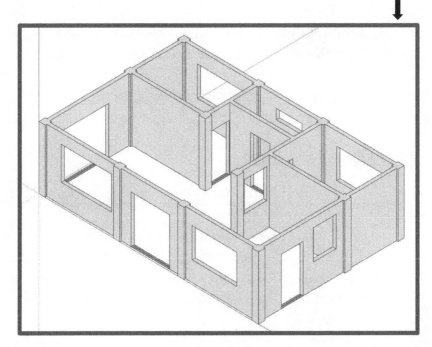

- With the walls complete, make them into a Group.
- Create a Layer named WALLS and using the Entity Info option put onto the Walls layer.

Practice

- **You now need to go back and practice the methods shown on creating the holes in the walls.**
- To do this –
  - o **Undo back until the sliding door and bedroom/bathroom door openings are filled in.** (Because the methods used are similar to those used for the windows there is no need to undo back to the window openings).
  - o **Using the methods shown produce the holes in the walls for those Door frames.**
  - o **Repeat until you can do it without referring to the instruction.**
  - o On completion, your model will be the same as that shown above.
  - o **Remember to Group and Put on to the Walls Layer.**
  - o **Save the model then exit SketchUp.**

Before putting in the Windows, Door Frames, and Doors you can have a look at two methods of producing a Roof.

How Do I Create a Roof

- There is a wide number of styles of roof available but the style will fall into two main types
  - o **Flat Roofs** – where the angle of slope does not exceed 10°. Used where the building shape is of irregular design and covers a large area. Usually made from wood or concrete and then covered with some form of covering material.

o **Pitched Roofs** – where the roof slope can vary from 15° up to 45°. Used on family dwellings where the building is of a regular shape. Usually constructed from wood or metal (aluminium or galvanized steel) and then covered with slates or tiles.

- For the **Bungalow - Project 1** we will have a **look at** two styles of **Pitched Roof** –
    o **Hip - Where all the sides (pitch) slope downwards to the walls.**

    o **Gable - Where two sides slope downwards and the other two sides join with the walls to produce a vertical face.**

Construction of a Simple Hip Roof

- Open the **Bungalow - Project 1** model.
    o Make sure the **Reference layout** is **OFF**
        - Turn the **Axes OFF**

    o Double pick the walls to **produce the Bounding Box,** then using the **Push/Pull** tool, **stretch** the **walls by 400mm** to simulate the top of the roof beam.

    o Pick the **Top view icon**

    o Using the **Rectangle tool** – draw a rectangle from the **bottom left corner of the bottom left column to the top right corner of the top right column - page 252.**

    o **Turn the Walls layer OFF.**
    o Pick the **Front-Right Iso** view.

Using the Rectangle Tool

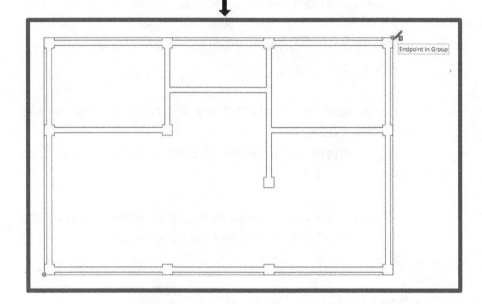

o **Offset the rectangle outwards by 750mm.**

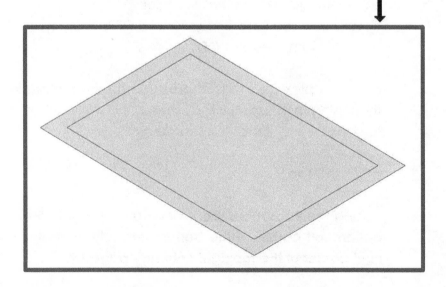

o **Erase the inner lines.**
o Using the **Line tool – draw two diagonal lines.**

The Basics - Part Two

View after the Diagonal lines have been drawn

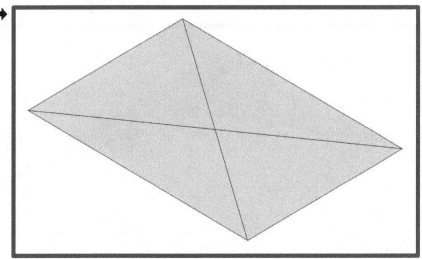

o Select the **Move tool and position it at the intersection** of the **two diagonal lines**

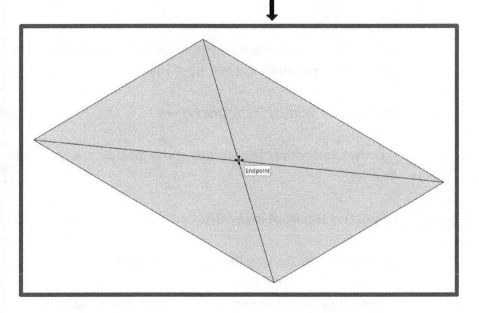

Endpoint

o **Pick and then drag up 2250mm on the Blue axis -**

Using the Move Tool to create the Hip Roof

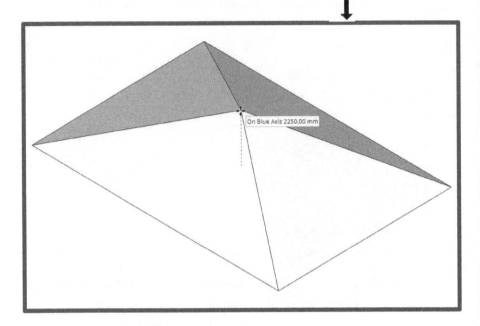

o Turn the roof into a Group.
o Create a Layer named HIP Roof and using the Entity Info option put onto the Hip Roof layer.

- **To create the Facia/Soffit board**

    o Draw another rectangle the same size as the roof outline.

    o Turn the **Hip Roof layer Off.**

    o **Offset** the rectangle **inwards** by **250mm.**

    o **Push/Pull** the inner rectangular area down **300mm.**

    o **Push/Pull** the outer rectangular area down **50mm.**

Creating the Facia/Soffit Board

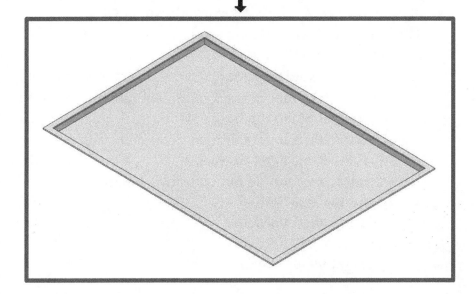

o Turn into a **Group.**
o **Create a Layer named Facia/Soffit and using the Entity Info option put the group onto the Facia/Soffit layer.**
o Put the **Hip Roof Layer** back **On.**
o Put the **Walls layer** back **On.**

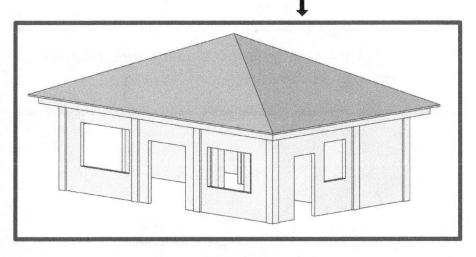

Construction of a Simple Gable Roof

- Turn the **Hip Roof** and the **Facia/Soffit Layer OFF.**
- Create a **new layer – Gable Roof.**
  - o Pick the **Top View icon –**
  - o Using the **Rectangle tool** – draw a rectangle from the **bottom left corner of the bottom left column to the top right corner of the top right column.**
  - o Turn the **Walls layer OFF.**
  - o Pick the **Front-Right Iso view.**
  - o **Offset** the rectangle **outwards** by **750mm.**
  - o **Erase the inner lines.**
  - o Pick the **Right View icon –**

View From the Right Viewpoint ⌐

o Pick the **Protractor tool** from the **Tape Measure tool group** and **position as shown – Pick ⌐**

Endpoint

o **Move the arrow to the right – Pick**

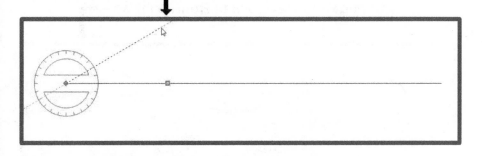

o **Move up** (a Guide Line appears) **until the Angle shows 30°**

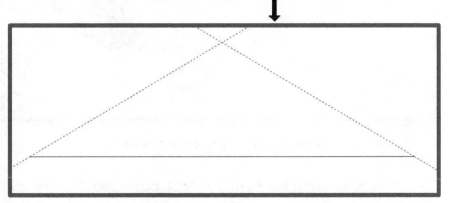

o **Pick.**
o **Repeat for the other end –**

o Using the **Line tool, the angled guidelines, draw the shape of the profile of the roof –**

Using the Line Tool to Draw the Profile of the Roof

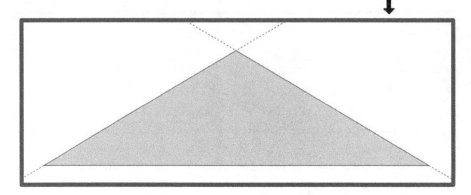

o **Change** the **viewpoint to Front-Right Iso** –

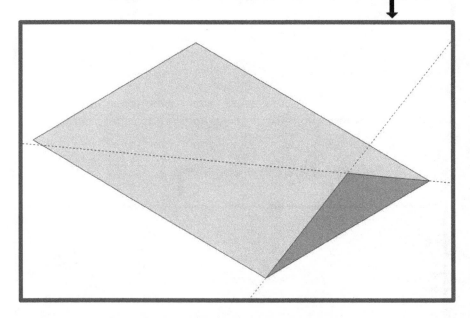

o Use the **Push/Pull tool to form the roof** –

o **After using the Push/Pull Tool, page 260, the roof over-hangs the walls by 750mm and to produce a gable end that is in-line with the end walls you need to produce a Facia/Soffit board.**

After Using The Push/Pull Tool ⌐

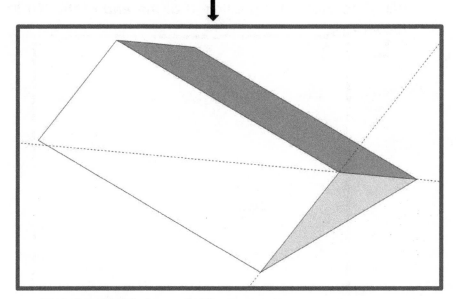

- Pick the **Right viewpoint icon.**
- Using the **Line tool** draw a horizontal line **250mm long from the bottom left corner** ⌐

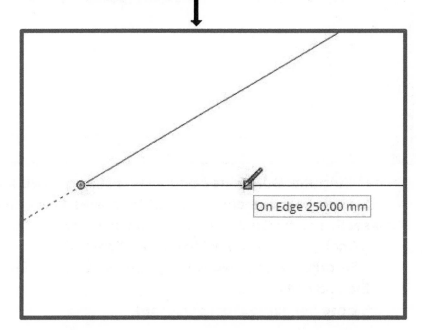

On Edge 250.00 mm

- **Repeat for the bottom right corner.**
- Using the **protractor positioned at the end of the left line drawn –**

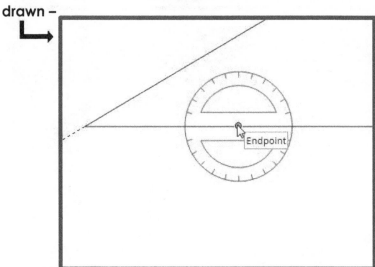

- o produce a **guideline at an angle of 30° -**
- o **Repeat for the bottom right line drawn**

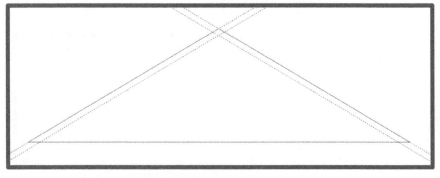

- o Using the **Guidelines and Line tool, draw two lines starting from the end of the 250mm lines to the intersection of the Guidelines, as shown on page 262.**
- o **Change** the **Viewpoint to a Front-Right Iso.**
- o **Re-adjust your viewpoint** so you have a better view of **the end of the roof.**
- o **Erase the outside roof guidelines.**

The Basics - Part Two

Using the Line Tool from the end of the 250mm lines ⌐

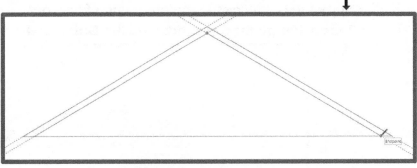

o **Position the Push/Pull tool as shown** ⌐

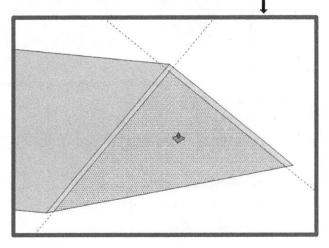

o **Push back 750mm –**

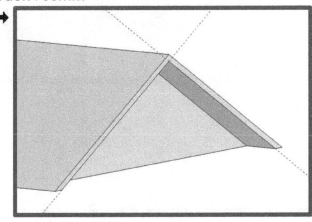

- Repeat for the other end of the roof –
  - o Copy the guidelines to the other end of the roof.
  - o Repeat the method of producing the Gable End.

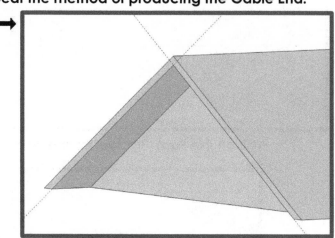

  - o **Erase the Roof guidelines.**
  - o Turn the **roof into a Group.**
  - o Using the **Entity Info** option **put onto the Gable Roof layer.**
  - o Turn the **Wall Layer ON.**
  - o Your model looks like –

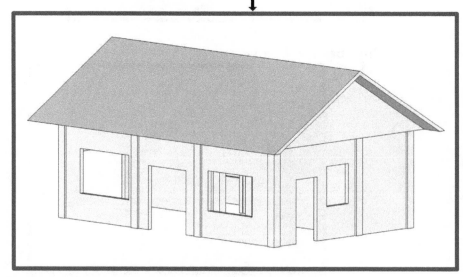

- You now need to put in the terrace wall and a floor.
    - Put the **Ref drawing back on** by picking **Scenes - Layout ON.**
    - Make sure the **Hip and Gable Roof layers are Off as well as** the **Facia/Soffit board layer.**
    - **Change** the **Viewpoint to a Front-Left Iso.**
        - Turn the **Axes OFF**
    - Using the **Line tool put in the Terrace walls – Push/Pull** to a height of **1000mm**

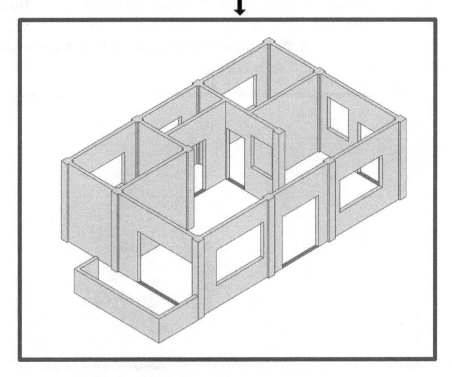

- **Group the Terrace Wall and then -**
    - **Create a Terrace wall layer** and **using Entity Info** put **the Terrace Wall onto** the **Terrace wall layer.**

To Create the Apron Floor –
- **Change** the **Viewpoint to Front-Right Iso.**

o Create a **New layer – Apron Floor.**
o Using the **Rectangle tool** – draw a rectangle from the **bottom left corner of the bottom left column to the top right corner of the top right column.**
o **Turn Off all the layers except Layer 0.**
o **Offset** the Rectangle **750mm outward.**
o **Erase** the **inner rectangular lines.**
o Then Push/Pull **Down 150mm.**
o **Turn the floor into a Group.**
o **Using the Entity Info** option put onto **the Apron Floor layer.**
o Turn the **Wall, Terrace Wall and Apron Floor Layers ON.**
o Your model looks like⌐

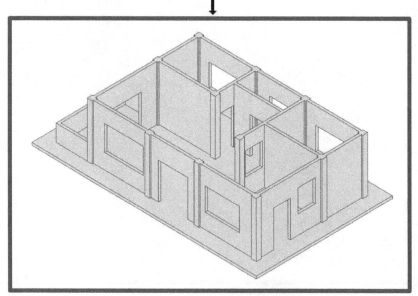

- **The Terrace area needs to be covered.**
  o Go to a **Left View viewpoint.**
  o **Draw two vertical guidelines 75mm in from the outside edges of the two columns - see page 266.**
  o **From the top edge of the two columns, draw two Horizontal guidelines 500mm and 750mm - see page 266.**

The Vertical and Horizontal Guidelines ⌐

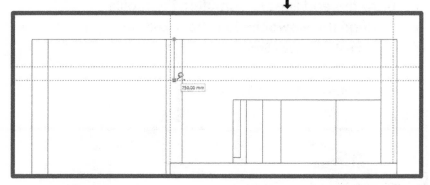

- **Zoom in to give a closer view of the guidelines and columns.**
- You may have to adjust your view so that you can see clearly the four guidelines.
- Using the **Line tool** – draw a line from the **left intersection of the top horizontal guideline to the right intersection of the top horizontal guideline.** ⌐

- Using the **3Point Arc tool** – draw an arc from the left Intersection of the second horizontal guideline to the midpoint of the top line just drawn to the right intersection of the second horizontal guideline ⌐

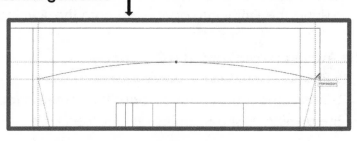

- **Erase the top line** then **Offset the arc 15mm down.**
- **Draw the end lines to complete the profile.**
- **Change the viewpoint to a Front-Left Iso.**
  - Push/Pull 2675mm.

  - **Remove the Guidelines**

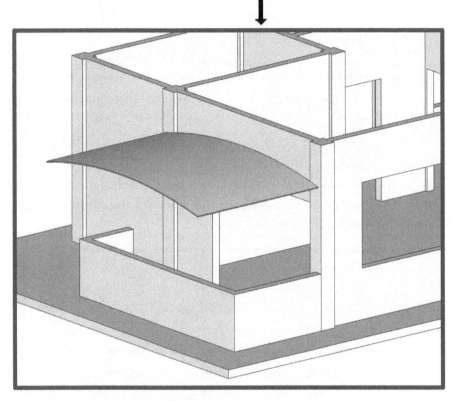

  - Turn the awning (cover) into a Group.
  - Create an Awning layer.
  - Using the **Entity Info** option **put onto the Awning layer.**

- **The Awning (cover) needs a 5° slope.**
  - Pick the **Front View icon** viewpoint.
  - Select the **Rotate tool** and **position at the midpoint of the awning** as shown on page 268, then **Pick.**

The Basics - Part Two

Position of the Rotate Tool

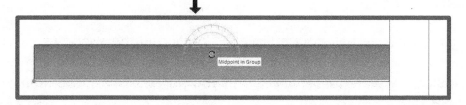

o **Move either horizontally left or right** (you get the message – **On Edge in Group**) – **pick.**
o Enter the angle of **(-5°).**

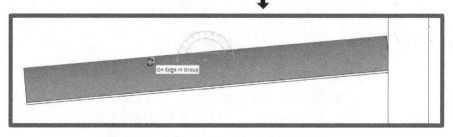

o **Move** the awning **110mm to the Right.**
o To finish put the **Hip Roof and Facia/Soffit Board layers back on.**

o **Save the Model.**

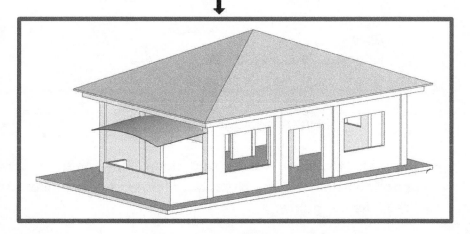

How Do I Put in the Windows, Door Frames and Doors.

You now need to concentrate on putting in the windows, door frames and doors. **In Part 1 you created your own 3D warehouse called My Warehouse, into which you put windows, door frames and doors based on the information given on pages 62 and 63.** You also placed in your **My Warehouse,** objects that you **imported from the 3D Warehouse.**

- To remind ourselves of the sizes of the windows, door frames doors and door handle used in *Project 1 - Bedroom Layout in Part One* ⅂

  o **Double Window Frame –**
    - Single External Size = **1175 x 1350 x 150**
    - Internal Size = **1117.5 x 1275 x 150**
    - Height from Floor = **950**
      (See Drawing page 100).

  o **Basic Door Frame –**
    - External Size = **1000 x 2150 x 150mm**
    - Internal Size = **900 x 2100 x 150mm**

  o **Door -**
  o Door Size - **900 x 2150 x 50**
  o Door Handle - **ϕ75 x 200mm**
    - Height From Floor **1150mm**
    - In from the Edge **100mm**

- **The windows, door frames and doors, now need to be imported from your, *My Warehouse* folder and then altered to suit the bungalow.**

- **As you don't need the following layers –**
  - **Roof.**
  - **Facia/Soffit Board.**
  - **Apron Floor.**
  - **Terrace Wall.**
  - **Awning.**
- Turn them **OFF.**

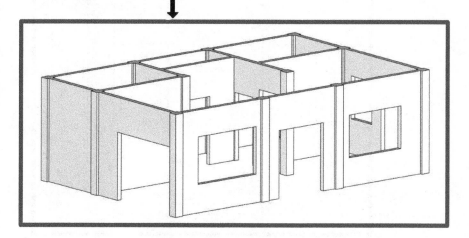

- Pick the **Top View** viewpoint icon then
  - **Save and Close the Model.**

Producing the Transom Frame for the Front Door

- For the Transom Frame, you will have to create a new model using the information shown on page 270

- Start a **NEW Drawing in your - My Warehouse Folder.**

- Set the **Drawing Environment.**

- Use a Style of **Shaded with Textures.**

- Using the information shown **produce the Transom frame,**

The Basics - Part Two

2D Drawing of the Transom Frame

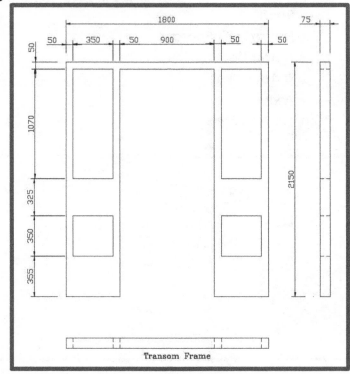

Transom Frame

3D Model of the Transom Frame

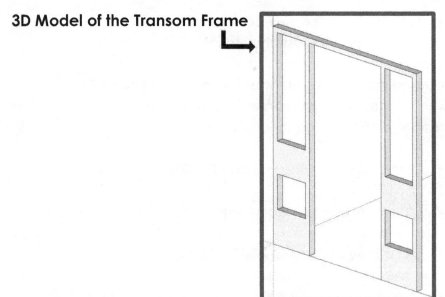

The Basics - Part Two

- Where the **glass panels** are go **put in the 5x10 mm grooves.**

- As you are going to **subtract** the glass form tool you will have to use the **Intersect Faces - With Model option.**

- Remember to **Group and copy a small and large Glass panel form tool so you can use them to form the groove and glass panels.**

- Put the **form tools in position** and use the **Solid subtract** then - **Intersect Faces - With Model.**

- **Delete the form tools**

- **Push/Pull each 5mm area to a depth of 10mm to create the grooves.**

- **Make the Transom Frame a Group.**

- **Create a Transom Frame Layer** and **then** put onto this layer using Entity Info.

- Use the **two form tools you have copied to produce the 4 glass panels, Group, then put onto a Glass Panel layer.**

- **Move into position** and then

  o From the **material library select - Glass and Mirrors.**
  o **Apply the blue translucent glass to each panel.**

The Basics - Part Two

Glass Applied to one of the grooved panels.

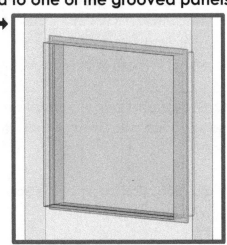

Glass Applied to the Transom Frame

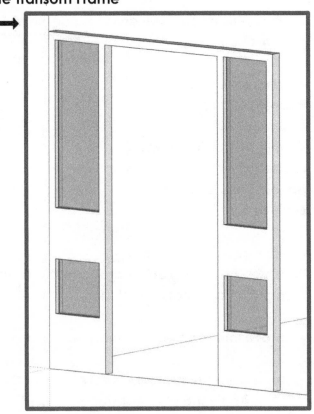

- **You now need to change the name of the model.**
- Select the **Model Name** in the Home Bar - **Transom Frame 1800 x 2150 x 75**
  - o This produces the **Enter A Model Name** edit box.
  - o Enter the name - **Transom Frame+Glass 1800x2150x75**
  - o Then pick the **OK** button.

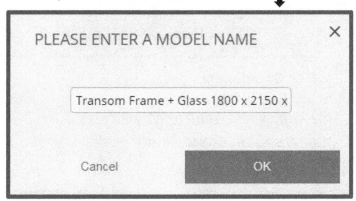

- **Save the Transom Frame Model then close.**

We can now start to insert the Door Frames, Doors and Windows from the - My Warehouse folder. Let's start with the Transom Frame Model.

- ˮOpen the **Bungalow - Project 1** model.
  - o Make sure you are in a **Top View viewpoint.**

To Insert the Transom Frame from My Warehouse.

- Pick the **File Icon in the Home Bar** and **from the options shown -**
  - o **Pick Insert.**
  - o This produces the **Insert File Box.**
  - o Pick **Trimble Connect.**
  - o This takes you to the **Insert File Page.** The file that we want is in the **My Warehouse folder** so -
  - o Pick **My Warehouse.**

- Scroll and select the -
  - o **Transom Frame + Glass 1800 x 2150 x 75** File.
  - o This produces

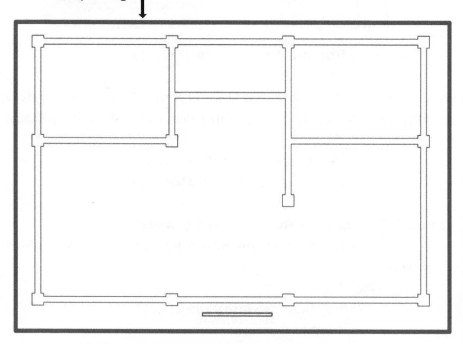

  - o Pick **Component.**
  - o The Bungalow - Project 1 Top View is returned with the **Transom Frame attached to the cursor.**
  - o Move to an **approximate position by the main door Opening.**

  - o Pick a **Front-Right Iso view,** viewpoint.

  - o **Move the Transom Frame into position.**

- **3D Model of the Transom Frame Moved into Position.**

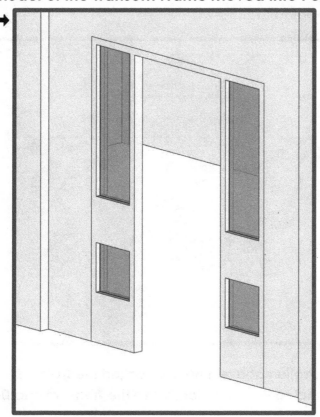

- **Insert the other door frames from the warehouse and place in approximate position**

- **For the Bedrooms and Bathroom, just Import one Internal Door Frame and adjust if necessary and then copy for the other two.**

- You will have to **use the Rotate tool to get them in-line** with the openings in the walls.

- It will also help when placing the Door Frames **to have the X-Ray mode on.**

- After putting the Door Frames in place the model will look similar to that shown

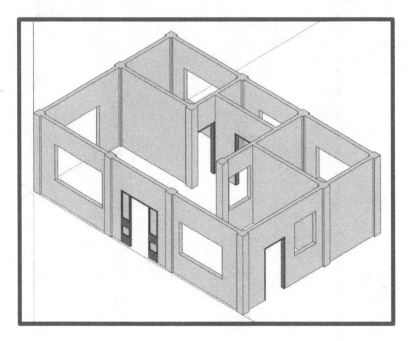

In the illustration above, I have checked the *Colour by Layer* in the layers panel so you can clearly see the Transom and Door frames.

- The methods used for the Door Frames can now be used on the Windows and Doors.

Inserting Windows

As mentioned above, when inserting objects you can either use the 3D warehouse or use previously constructed objects you have created and put in a separate folder called - **My Warehouse.** I have assumed you have put the window frames, door frames, doors and door handle produced in the **Dining Room** and **Bedroom layouts** from **Part One** into **your own warehouse folder.** I also added the panes of glass to my window frames to complete the windows.

To Complete the Windows By Adding the Glass Panes -

- Open the **Double Window Frame 2350 x 1350 x 150, from your - My Warehouse folder.**
- Change the view to, **Right View**
  - o **Put X-Ray mode on -** this shows the groove in the casement.

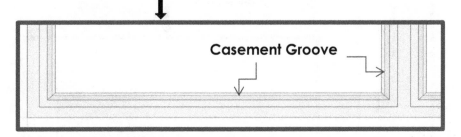

Casement Groove

- Using the **Rectangle Tool - draw a rectangle from the bottom left corner of the casement groove to the top right corner of the casement groove.**

- **Repeat** for the **other window frame.**
- Turn the Window Frame layer **OFF**
- Change the Viewpoint to a **Front-Right**
- **Push/Pull the two rectangles rectangles 5mm left.**

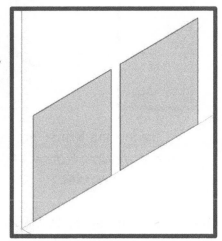

- **Group** each rectangle.

- **Create a layer called Window Glass.**
- **Use Entity info and put onto the Window Glass layer.**
- **Change the Viewpoint to Top.**
- **Put the Window Frame layer ON.**

- **Check to see if the glass pane is in the correct position.**

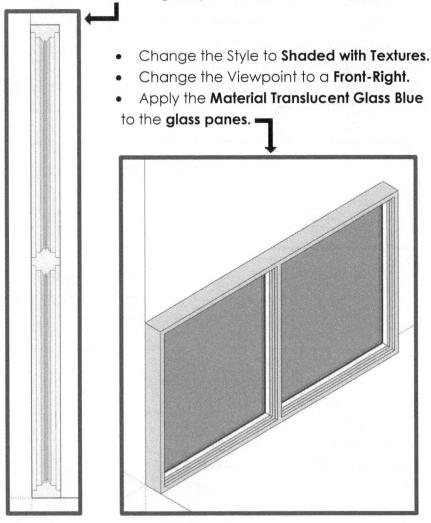

- Change the Style to **Shaded with Textures.**
- Change the Viewpoint to a **Front-Right.**
- Apply the **Material Translucent Glass Blue** to the **glass panes.**

- **Change the Name** of the Model to -
Double Window Frame + Glass 2350 x 1350 x 150.
- **Save the Model.**

The window is ready to be inserted into the Bungalow
- **Open** the **Bungalow - Project 1** model.
- Change the Viewpoint to - **Top View.**

- Insert the Double Window Frame + Glass model and place in approximate position.

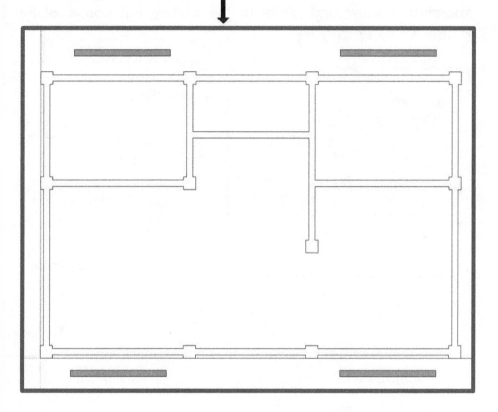

Action Plan

1. Change the Viewpoint to, Front-Right.
2. Start with the Lounge Window and put in place.
3. Use the Scale tool to adjust to the height.
4. Repeat for the Dining and Bedroom windows.

Action Plan 1 and Action Plan 2

- Change the Viewpoint to Front Right.
- Zoom in on the Lounge window area.

Action Plan 2 Continued

- Using the Move tool pick the bottom left corner of the imported window and move to the bottom left corner of the lounge window cavity ⌐

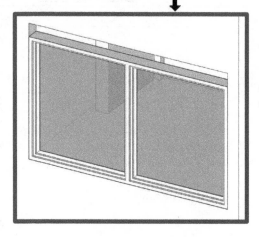

Action Plan 3

Adjusting the height of the window frame.

- The window frame is **OK lengthways** but is **too small height ways,**

- Pick the **X-Ray icon.**

- Pick the **Scale tool.** ⌐

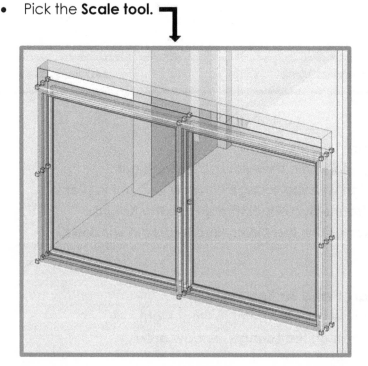

The Basics - Part Two

- Pick the **Top centre grip.**

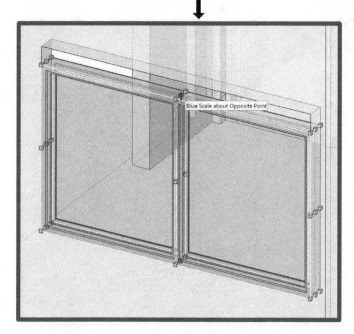

- Pull up onto the top edge of the window opening – Pick

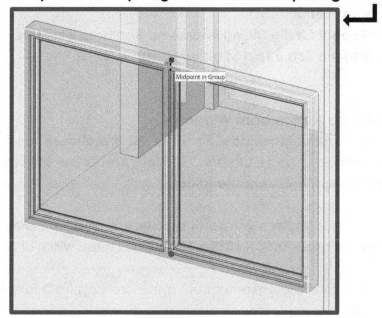

- Pick the **Select tool.**

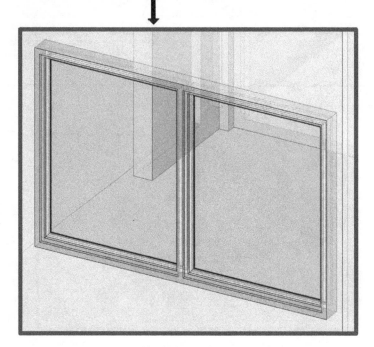

Action Plan 4
- **Repeat for the Dining Room and Bedroom windows.**
- **Use the Scale Tool to adjust for the LENGTH.**

The Kitchen & Bathroom Windows
We could select a window from the 3D Warehouse for the two kitchen windows and bathroom, **but let's create our own and then copy it to the My Warehouse folder.**

- For the **kitchen windows produce a basic window frame** having sizes of **1050 x 1350 x 150 with a Frame width of 37.5mm.**

- Produce the **casement** using the drawing **from Part 1 page 101.**

Window Frame with Casement

- **Put the glass in the frame by using the same method as for the Double Window Frame.**

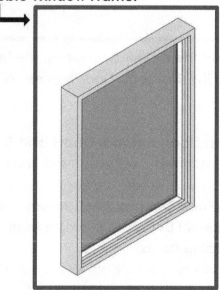

- **Move/Copy into the holes in the wall.**

- **Copy to the Bathroom & Scale.**
- Now **copy** the Window Frame and Glass to your **MY Warehouse.**
- Use a name like **- Single window frame 1050x1350x150.**
- The Bungalow will look the same as that shown

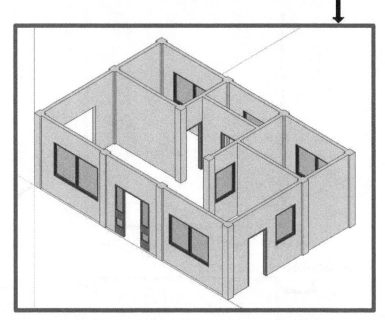

Again, I have checked the *Colour by Layer* in the layers panel so you can clearly see the Transom, Door frames, Window Frames and the Glass Panels.

Inserting the Transom Door, Internal Doors and Door Handle .
- Use the **same methods** as used on **the Windows and Door Frames.**
    - o Use the **6 Panel Door** For the **Transom Door.**
    - o For the **Internal Doors** use the **Plain Door.**
- **Kitchen and Sliding Doors**
    - o We will have to **create both Kitchen and Sliding Doors** from the **information given** and put them into the **My Warehouse folder.**

- Start with the **Kitchen Door** which is to have **two Glass panels.**

Kitchen Door Details

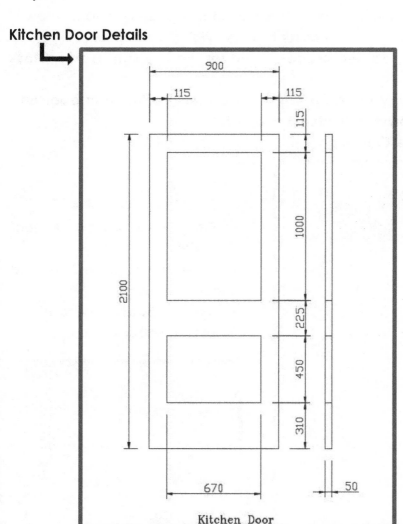

Kitchen Door

- **Start a NEW SketchUp model in the My Warehouse Folder.**
- Set the **Drawing Environment.**
- Use a Style of **Shaded with Textures.**
- **Using the** information shown **produce the Kitchen Door Frame.**

- Where the **glass panels** are to go **put in the 5x10 mm grooves.**
- As you are going to **subtract** the glass form tool you will have to use the **Intersect Faces - With Model option.**
- **Repeat the process used for the Transom Frame Glass Panels.**
- **Copy the door handle used for the Transom door and position as indicated on page 123.**
- **The Kitchen door will look the same as that shown.**

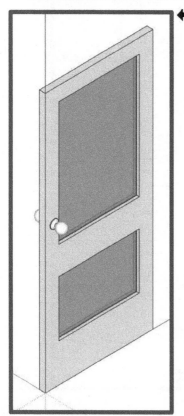

- **Save the model.**
- **Open the Bungalow - Project 1 model.**
- **Insert the Kitchen Door and place in position.**
- **Use the Scale tool to fit the door in the door frame.**

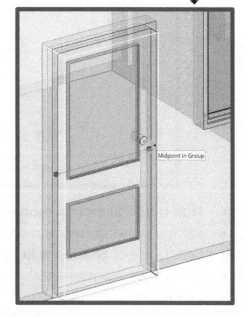

Completed Kitchen Door in Position ⌐

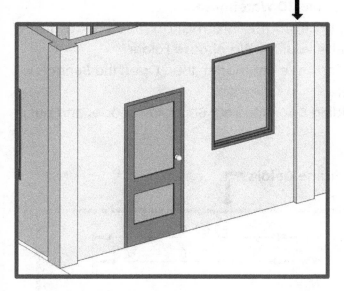

- **Notice that the Layers associated with the inserted model are also inserted.**

Your model now looks like -
⌐→

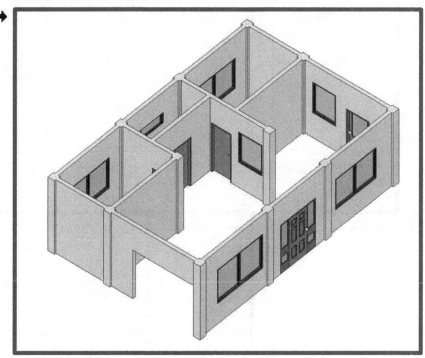

- For the Sliding Door, you can **use the information shown** or **use a model from the 3D Warehouse.**
- If constructing from the information given, **start a NEW SketchUp model in your My Warehouse Folder.**
- On completion **Save the model,** then **Open the Bungalow - Project 1** model.
- **Insert the Sliding Door** into your Bungalow model and **put in position.**

Sliding Door Outer Frame Details

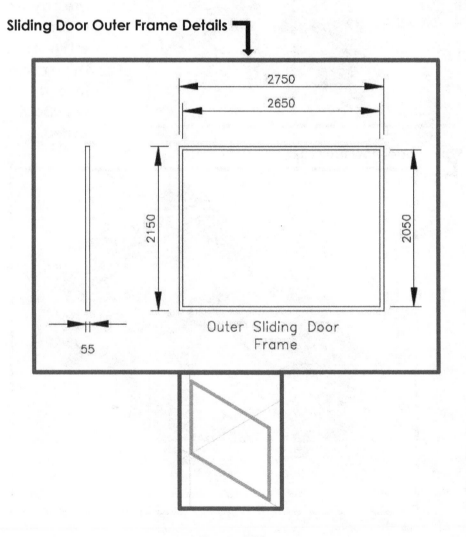

Outer Sliding Door Frame

Sliding Door Inner Frame

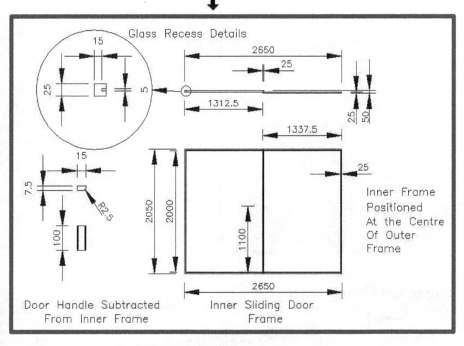

Glass Recess Details

Door Handle Subtracted
From Inner Frame

Inner Sliding Door
Frame

Inner Frame
Positioned
At the Centre
Of Outer
Frame

Glass Pane Size For Inner Frame

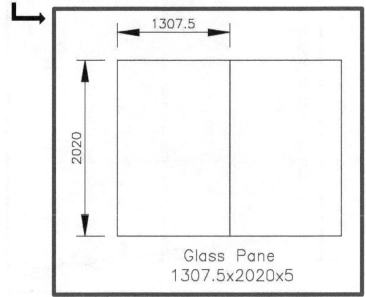

Glass Pane
1307.5x2020x5

Glass Pane to Fit in Inner Frame Recess

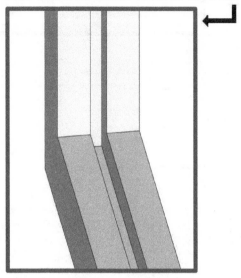

Completed Sliding Door

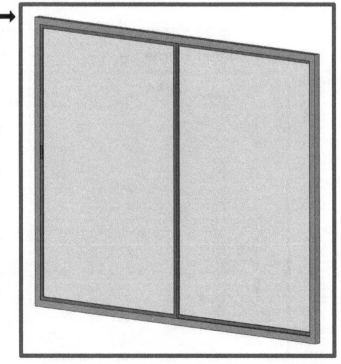

- On completion of importing and positioning the doors **put the Terrace Wall layer ON.** Your Bungalow will be similar to that shown –

Front-Left Iso viewpoint of the Bungalow

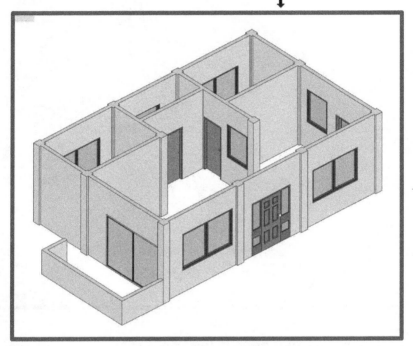

- **The Terrace walls need to be joined to the main walls of the Bungalow** through the use of the Solid Tools Option - **Union, as shown on page 292,**

How Do I Tidy Up the Layer Pane

Over the course of developing the Bungalow, we have created a lot of layers. The layers are all mixed up so when looking for a particular layer you have to scroll through all of them to locate the one you want. To overcome this problem you can use the Ascend/Descend Icon which will put the layers in Alphabetical order.

The Basics - Part Two

Union of the Walls and Terrace Wall.

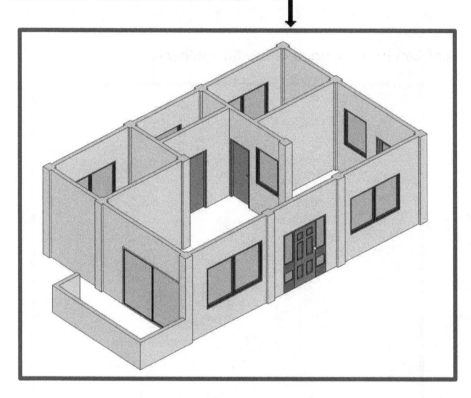

- **Open the Layer pane in the Panel Bar.**
- **Scroll down to the bottom of the pane** and pick the **Ascend/Descend icon.**

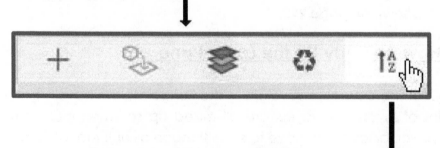

- **The Layers are placed in Alphabetical order with the layers starting with the letter A at the top, as shown, or from the bottom up.**

The Basics - Part Two

Layers Placed in Alphabetical Order

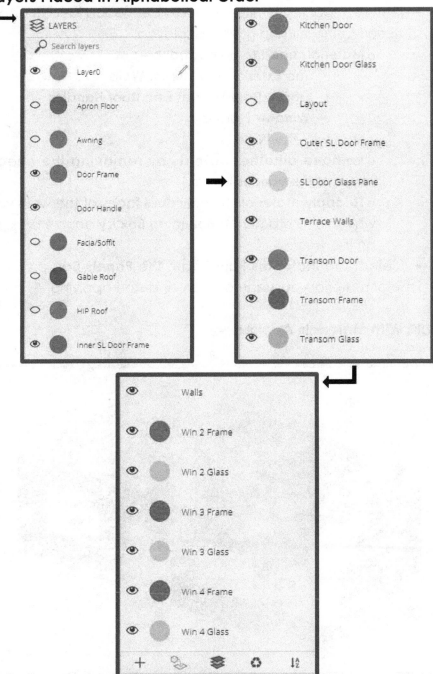

Applying Materials -

- Before importing furniture it would be a good idea to apply materials to the varying groups displayed.
  - o **Materials need to be added to –**
    - **The Exterior and Interior Walls**
    - **Doors, Door Frames and Door Handles**
    - **Window Frames**
  - o Start with the **Walls.**
  - o **Remove all other objects by removing the check marks of the various layers.**
  - o **To apply materials to individual faces** of the walls you will have to **produce a Bounding Box** by double clicking on the walls.
- Select the **Materials Panel** from the **Panels Bar,** pick the type of material you want to apply and start applying –

Walls With Materials Applied ⌐

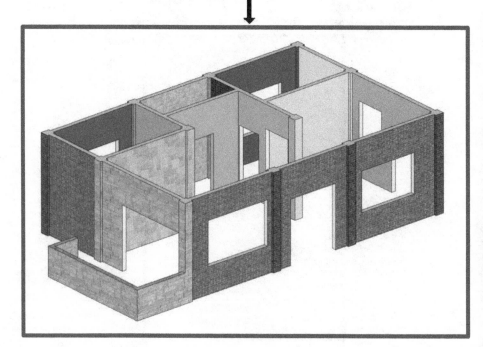

Applying Materials to other features

- With the materials added to the walls, you can **start applying materials to** the **Window Frames, Door Frames, Doors and Door Handles.**
- I am going to keep the same colour for all of the **exterior features - Transom Frame and Door, all of the Window Frames, the Kitchen Frame and Door and the Sliding Door Outer Frame.**
- It would be easier if the walls were removed so **turn the Walls layer OFF.**

- **Apply materials of your choice to the features mentioned.**

Materials applied to the above features. ⌐

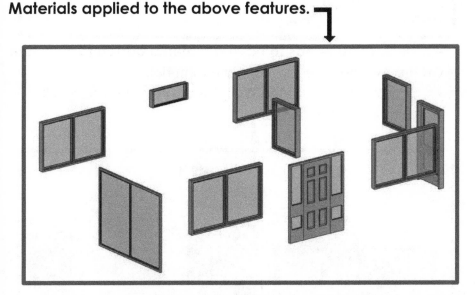

- You now can apply materials to the **Internal Door Frames, Internal Sliding Door Frame and Doors** and also the **Door Handles. I have changed the Glass Panels in the Sliding Door to Translucent Glass Tinted.**

- On completion, windows, doors, door frames and door handles will look similar to that shown –

The Basics - Part Two

Completed Windows, Door Frames, Doors and Door Handles

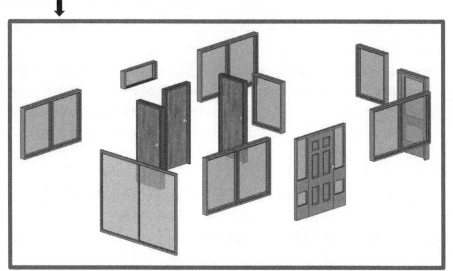

- The **Awning needs to have a material added to it,** so **turn ON the Awning layer** and **apply a material.**
- On completion put the **Walls layer ON.** Your model will look similar to the one shown.

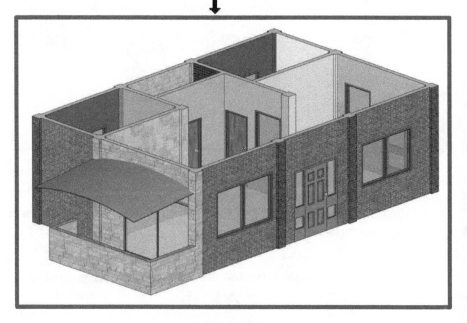

Floors

You now need to think about the floor. At the moment we have what is called an apron floor, what we need are individual floor areas. The best way of applying individual floor areas is by –

- **Turning All the layers OFF except Layer0 and the Layout layer.**

Drawn Layout

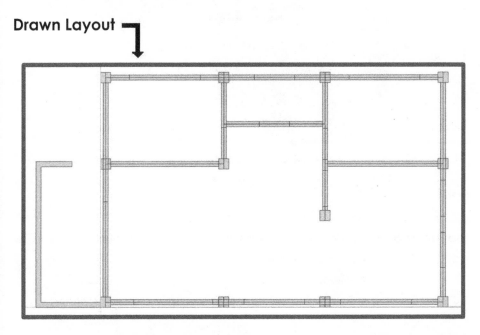

- Using the **Reference layer as a guide** and the **Line Tool,** produce **individual floor areas for the –**
    - o **Lounge**
    - o **Kitchen / Dining**
    - o **Bedrooms 1 and 2**
    - o **Comfort Room**
    - o **Terrace**

- **On producing the floor areas Push/Pull each area up 3mm.**
- **Apply a Material to each floor including the Apron floor.**

Materials Applied to Each Floor Area ⌐

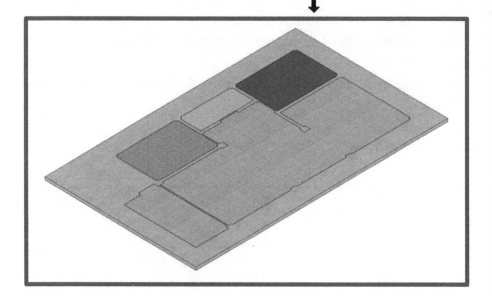

Roof

To **complete the exteriors** of the house **the roof needs to have roofing materials applied.** Also, **the Fascia/Soffit Board needs to have a Paint colour applied to it.**

- Open the **Hip Roof layer** and apply a **roofing material.**
- Open the **Fascia/Soffit layer** and apply a **paint colour.**

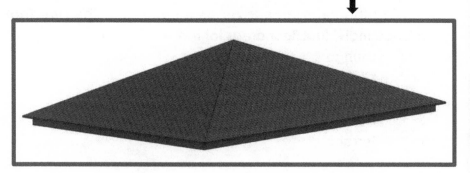

With the roof finished the exterior of the bungalow is complete. To have a look at the completed bungalow up to this point.

- Turn On all the relevant layers.

The Exterior of the bungalow will be similar to that shown.

Furniture
Using the furniture layout drawing as a guide (page 213) import from the 3D Warehouse the varying pieces of furniture. You can adjust the imported furniture to suit your layout by using the Scale tool.

Your completed design could look similar to the layout shown on page 213.

Varying 3D views of the model are shown on pages 300 to 303.

Completed Furniture Layout

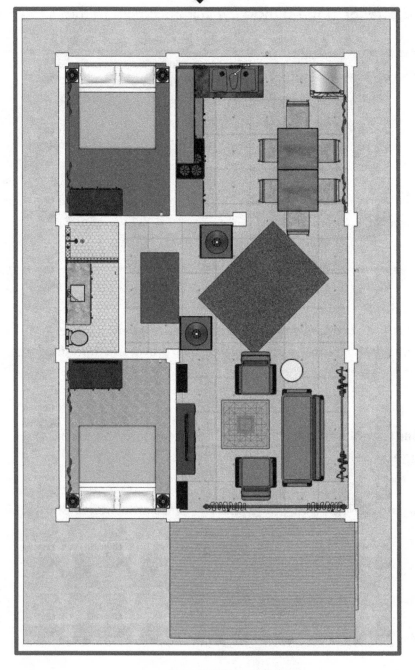

3D View – Without the Roof and Fascia/Soffit board

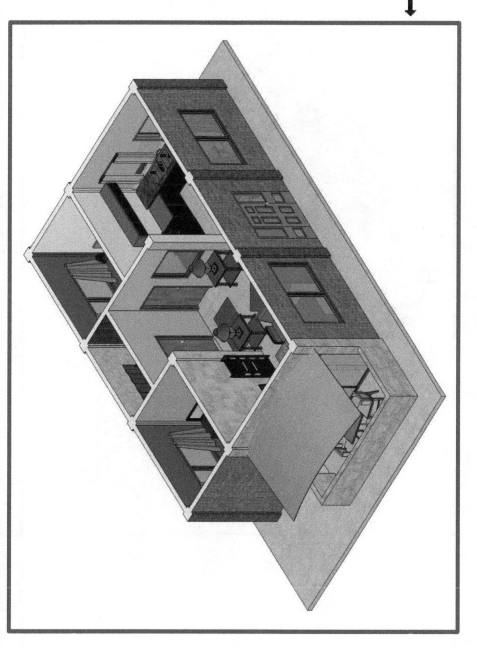

3D View – Without Walls and Awning ⌐

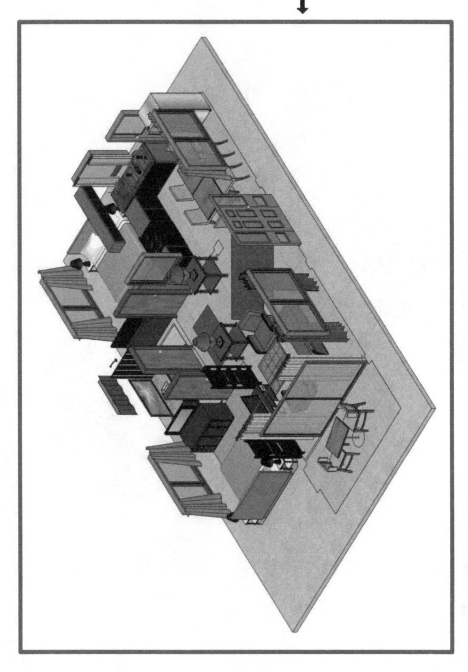

3D View - Looking From the Back of the Bungalow

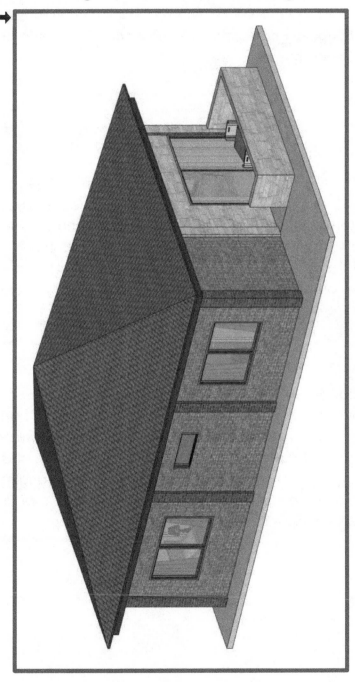

- **Save and then exit SketchUp Free**

With the bungalow completed you now need to put into practice what has been shown.

Bungalow 2

To get further practice into the use of SketchUp Free produce Bungalow 2 using the information shown. Produce the Layout, turn it into a Reference drawing and then proceed and produce your 3D model using the same methods and techniques shown.
Apply materials to the interior and exterior and complete the bungalow by putting in the furniture from your My Warehouse folder and/or the online 3D Warehouse.

Information For Bungalow 2

Two layout drawings are shown, one for the columns and walls, the other for the windows, door frames and doors. You will need to take into consideration the Roof design. The roof is not of a hip or gable design but is known as a Shed Roof with slope angles of 15° for both roofs. The information for producing the roof is given under the heading – Roof Information.

The Basics - Part Two

Column and Wall Layout Drawing

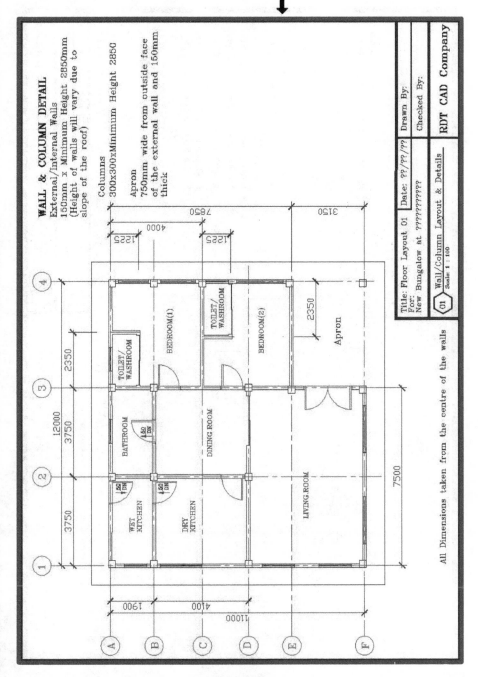

WALL & COLUMN DETAIL
External/internal Walls
150mm x Minimum Height 2850mm
(Height of walls will vary due to slope of the roof)

Columns
300x300xMinimum Height 2850

Apron
750mm wide from outside face of the external wall and 150mm thick

All Dimensions taken from the centre of the walls

Title: Floor Layout 01   Date: ??/??/??   Drawn By:
For:
New Bungalow at ??????????   Checked By:

01 Wall/Column Layout & Details
Scale 1 : 100

RDT CAD Company

BEDROOM(1)
TOILET/WASHROOM
BEDROOM(2)
TOILET/WASHROOM
BATHROOM
DINING ROOM
WET KITCHEN
DRY KITCHEN
LIVING ROOM
Apron

7850
4000
1225
1225
3150
2350
2350
12000
3750
3750
1900
4100
1900
11000
7500

Windows, Door Frame's and Doors Layout Drawing

Window, Door Frame/Door Layout & Information

D1 DOOR FRAME:
External Size:2100x2150x150
Internal Size:2000x2100x150

D1 DOOR:
1000x2100x50

D2 DOOR FRAME:
External Size:1000x2150x50
Internal Size:900x2100x150

D2 DOOR:
900x2100x50

D3 SLIDING DOOR FRAME:
External Size:2100x2150x50
Internal Size:2000x2050x50

D3 SLIDING DOOR:
External Size:1012.5x2050x25
Internal Size:987.5x2000x25

WINDOW(1):
2000x1400x150 Frame = 40mm
Height From Floor = 900mm

WINDOW(2):
1400x1500x150 Frame = 40mm
Height From Floor = 900mm

WINDOW(3):
1800x1350x150 Frame = 40mm
Height From Floor = 1100mm

WINDOW(4):
1000x1350x150 Frame = 40mm
Height From Floor =1100mm

WINDOW(5):
1000x450x150 Frame = 40mm
Height From Floor = 1900mm

WINDOW(6):
1300x1400x150 Frame = 40mm
Height From Floor = 900mm

WINDOW(7):
1500x1400x150 Frame = 40mm
Height From Floor = 900mm

All Dimensions taken from the centre of the walls

Title: Floor Layout 02
Date: ??/??/??
Drawn By:
For: New Bungalow at ?????:?????
Checked By:

02 Window/Door Layout & Details
Scale: 1 : 100

RDT CAD Company

Roof Information – Front Elevation

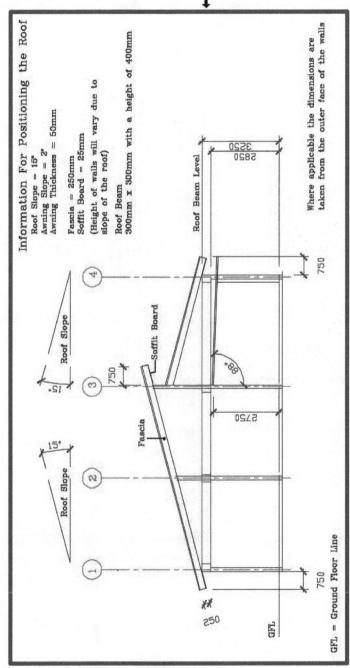

Roof Information – Right Elevation

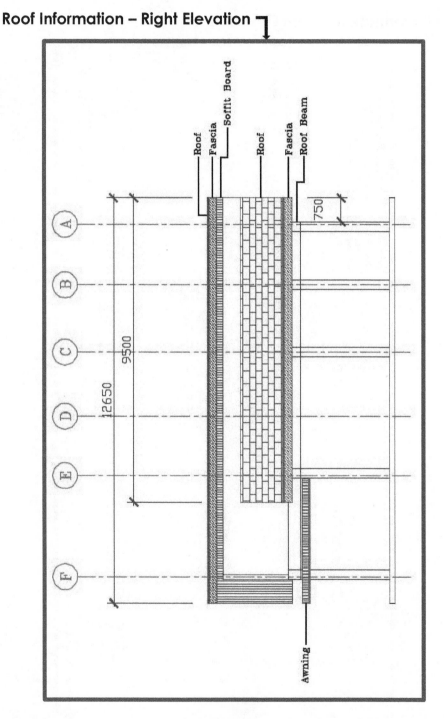

Action Plan For The Layout and Reference Drawing

- **Start SketchUp Free and set the environment.**
- Save as **Bungalow 2.**
- Start with the measuring tape tool to **layout the centre position of the walls.**
- Use the Line tool to **put in the centre line of the walls.**
- Delete the varying areas and **produce a 300x300 column** using the rectangle tool make it a **group and move/copy into position.**
- Use the measuring tape tool to **layout the walls.**
- Use the rectangle tool or the line tool to **put in the walls.**
- **Position the windows, and door frames** by using the tape measure tool to establish the centres and lengths of the windows and door frames, then use the rectangle tool to **produce their profiles.**
- Produce the **Reference Drawing.**
- **Save**

Layout Will Look Like -

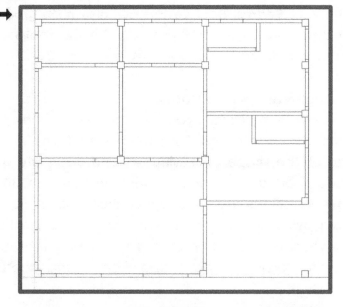

3D Model
Walls, Columns and Roof Beams

To produce the walls and columns use the methods shown and push/pull to a height of 2850mm.

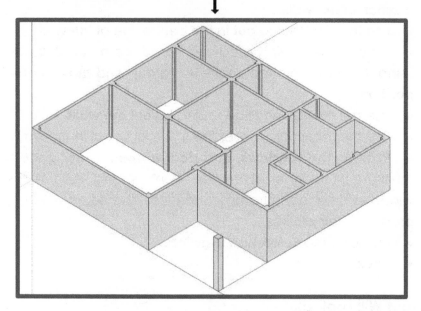

Produce the Roof Beams. Roof Beams are drawn on ground zero ready to be moved on top of the walls, Put the roof beams in position on top of the walls and columns. **see page 311.**

Windows, Door Frames and Doors

With the lower walls in position, you can start creating the gaps for the windows and door frames. **The shape of the holes in the walls will depend on the shape your windows and doors are going to take.** If you import a **non-standard window** from the **3D Ware-house, draw a profile of the window then Push/Pull to 150mm and use as your Window form tool.** With the holes in the walls completed you can start to insert from your My Warehouse/3D Warehouse the varying windows door frames and doors, page 312.

Roof Beam Constructed on ground zero ⌐

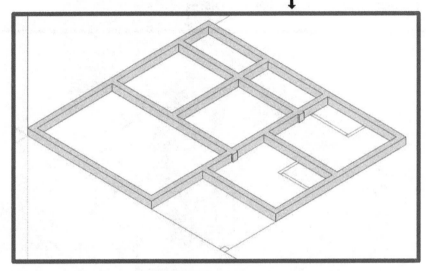

Roof Beams placed in position ⌐

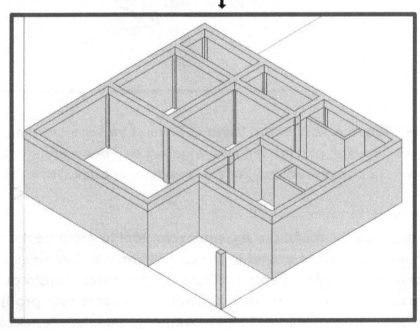

You will not be able to put the upper walls in position until you have the two roofs in place.

Doors and Windows placed in the wall cavities created by the door and window formtools.

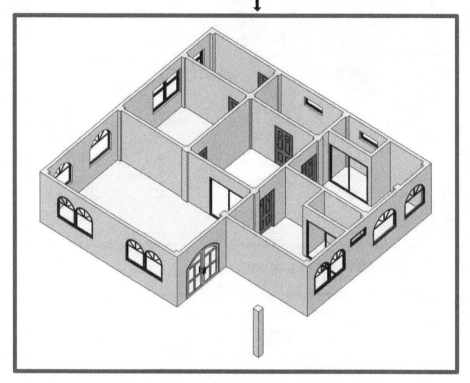

- Turn the Roof Beam Layer OFF whilst you are creating the wall cavities and inserting the windows and doors etc.
- On completion, put the Wall Beam layer back ON

The Roof

To produce the roofs, use the **protractor tool to produce the two 15° angles from the corner of the roof beam,** and the **measuring tool to produce the 50mm roof and 250mm fascia board guide lines.** Using the guide lines **produce the roofs end profiles,** remember to include the **750mm overhang, and then Push/Pull to 9500mm for the lower roof and 12650mm for the upper roof.** Your roofs and fascia boards should be similar to those shown.

Upper and Lower Roofs

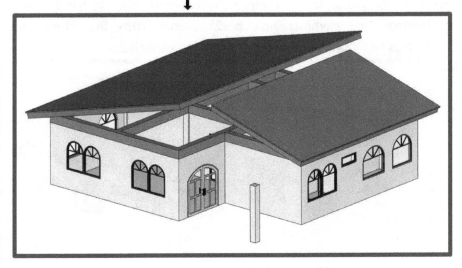

The Upper Walls and Roof Supports

With the two sloping roofs in position, the next step is to put in the Upper Walls and roof supports. **Using the slopes of the roofs as a guide and a wall thickness of 150mm create the upper walls and roof supports** as shown.

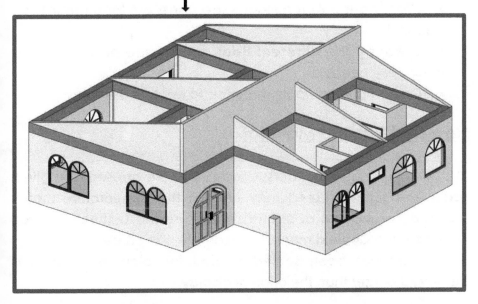

The Awning

You now can put in the Awning from the main door to the column. Remember **the awning has a 2° slope from the door and overhangs the column by 750mm in both directions.**

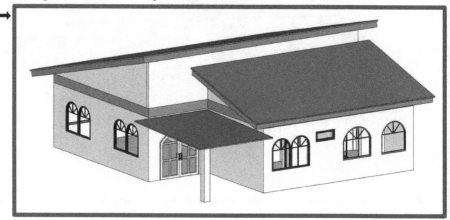

Completion of the Exterior and Interior

To complete the interior of your model you need to produce an **Apron floor** and **a floor for each of the rooms** using the method shown earlier.

- Creating the **Apron Floor - see page 264 for a reminder** if Needed.
- Creating the **different floor areas - see page 297 as a reminder** if needed.
- **On completion apply materials to each of the floors.**

How Do I Scale a Material

Materials, such as Tiles, Roofs, Carpets etc are **applied at a given scale.** The scale entered **may not suit the appearance that is required.** To alter the appearance you use the **Texture - Position Options** in the **Context menu.** For example, the carpet displayed in the lounge **has been scaled so that the diamond pattern is displayed bigger than the original display.**

The Basics - Part Two

The Original Display when Applied

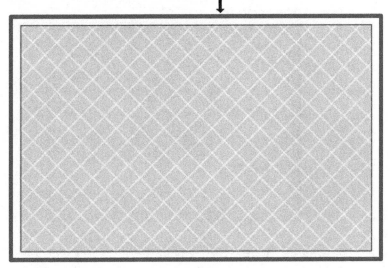

- **Pick the carpet and then Right click.**
- From the options displayed pick **Texture.**

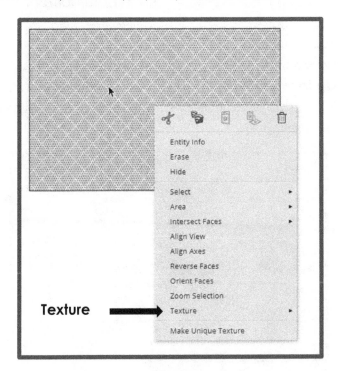

Texture ➡️

- Pick - **Position.**
- **Four pins appear** on the carpet

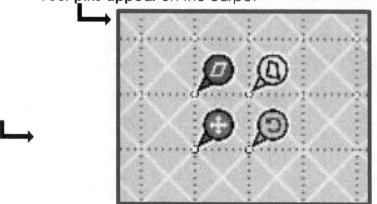

- The Blue and Green Pins will scale the selected material.
- The Blue Pin scales by stretching/shrinking in the Vertical direction.
- The Green Pin scales uniformly in both Horizontal and Vertical directions.
- Scroll in on the Four Pins
- **Hold down the Pick button on the Green pin** and **carefully drag to the RIGHT** until the pattern is **the size that you want.** The protractor indicates whether you are keeping in line.
- **After Scaling**

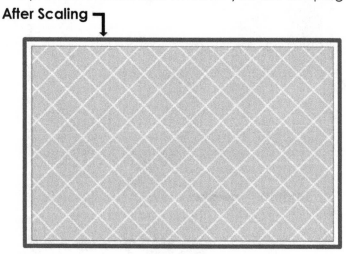

Materials can now be applied to the interior and exterior of the Bungalow. The look of your 3D model will largely depend on the type of windows and doors imported from the warehouse and the type of materials you have applied to the different features.

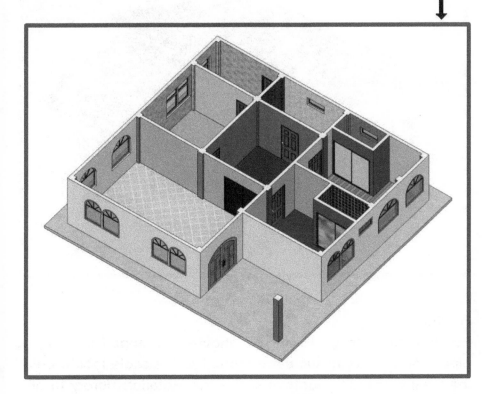

- **With the Interior and Exterior finished - Save your work.**
- **Get into the habit of saving on a regular basis and even exiting SketchUp Free.**

If you <u>have</u> exited SketchUp Free
- **Start SketchUp Free and Open the Bungalow 2 model.**

Apply the roofing materials.
- Use **Texture-Position** to **scale the roofing material** to achieve the effect you want.

The Two Roofs and Awning After the Roofing Materials have been applied and scaled.

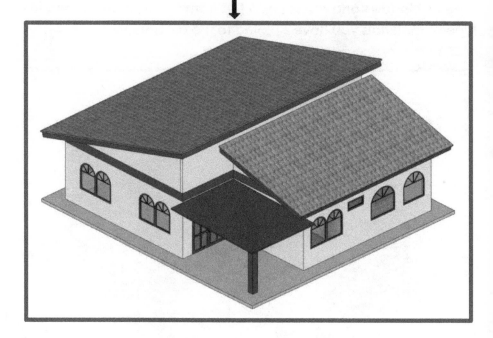

Furniture

You now need to go to the Warehouse and import the varying pieces of furniture to suit each room. Use the **scale tool to adjust the furniture to suit your layout.** Use the **Materials Library to alter the colour or fabrics** of the imported furniture. **Copy furniture from the Bungalow Project 1.**

Inserting, positioning, and scaling all the pieces of furniture takes time. Just remember to Save as you complete each room. On completing your furniture layout exit SketchUp Free.

Page 319 shows two views of how your model may look once you have applied furniture.

Furniture Applied to the Bungalow ⌐

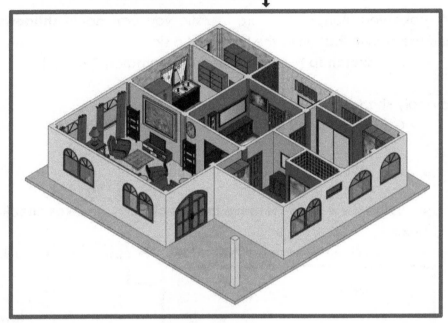

Another View of the Furniture layout. ⌐

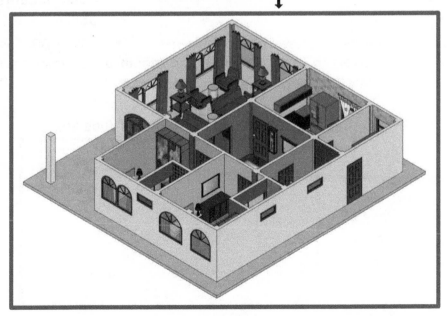

How Do I Create A More Realistic View

To make your Bungalow more realistic you can **apply shadows and use a style that gives the illusion of a sky.**

- **Start SketchUp Free and Open the Bungalow 2 model**

To apply shadows –

- Go to the **Panels Bar** and pick the **Display panel Icon** -

- In the **View Area** - **remove the check** from the **Axes check box.**
- Move down and pick the **Shadows OFF option to turn it ON.**

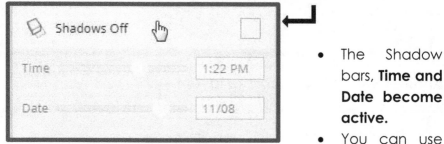

- The Shadow bars, **Time and Date become active.**
- You can use the **sliders to select the time and month** or you can enter the **time and date in the appropriate box.**

- For example - **10:00am** and the month of **June 2020**

This produces a view as shown ⌐

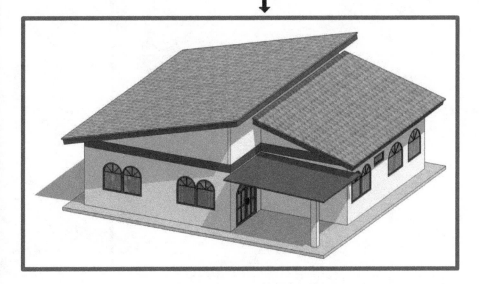

- **If your model** looks **Hazy** its because you have the **FOG setting ON**
  - o Turn the **Fog setting OFF.**
  - o **OR**
  - o **Move the Distance sliders to the ends of the bar.**

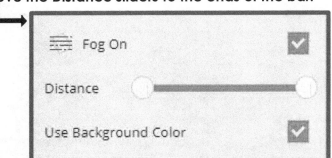

- **Then Turn the Fog Setting OFF**
- The use of the Fog setting lets you produce a **misty or hazy effect.**
- The **Fog setting ON** also gives access to the **Use Background Colour** colour pallet.

Background Colour Palette

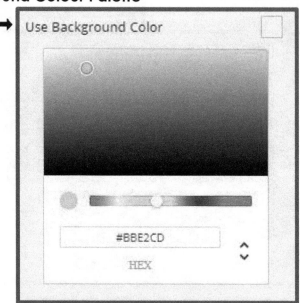

- Picking the check mark in the **Use Background Colour** checkbox enables you to choose a colour to apply to the model's background.

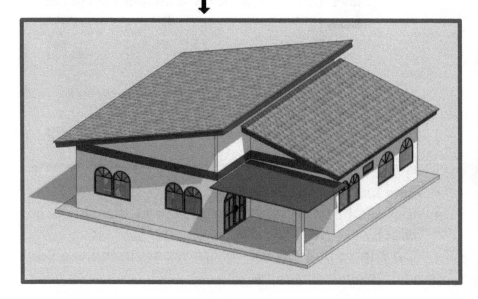

To Resemble the Sky.
- **Open the Styles Panel Icon.**
- Pick **Browse** and from the options shown pick the **Default Styles.**
- From the varying styles shown you want to select one that shows a **blue sky, either the - Simple Style or Urban Planning Style.** (In the illustrations that follow I have used the **Urban Planning Style**).
- **Open** the **Display Panel** and turn the **Axes OFF.**
- **Make sure the Fog setting is OFF**
- **Close the Display Panel.**
- **Open** the **View Panel** and pick **Perspective.**
- This produces a **perspective view of the Bungalow, but,** probably **no blue sky.**
- **Using** the **Orbit Tool - position at the bottom of the screen and orbit up.**
- The **blue sky appears** at the **top of the screen.**
- **To give a more even viewpoint** use the orbit tool so that **the horizon appears as shown.**

Another Realistic View

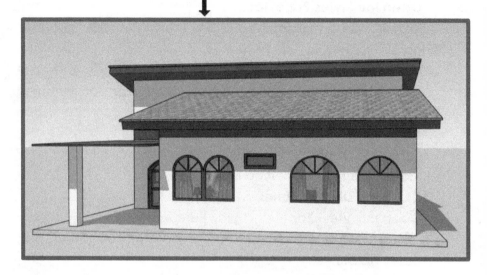

The Effect of using the Simple Style and turning the Fog Setting ON

The Simple Style produces a green ground. Turning the Fog Setting ON produces a softer merging of the sky and ground.

Your model could be enhanced further by importing backgrounds, using the sand-box tool to produce terrain, apply internal lighting, and rendering to make your model photo-realistic. The use of these advanced tools and techniques though are beyond the scope of this book.

How Do I Print My Model

It is assumed that you have your printer connected to your computer and configured to your windows operating system.

- **From** the **Home Bar**
  - o **Select** the **Files Icon**
    - ▪ From the options displayed pick - **Print**

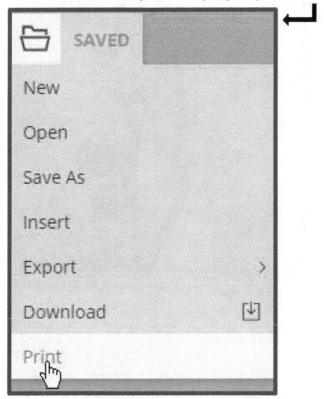

This produces the Print Preview screen.

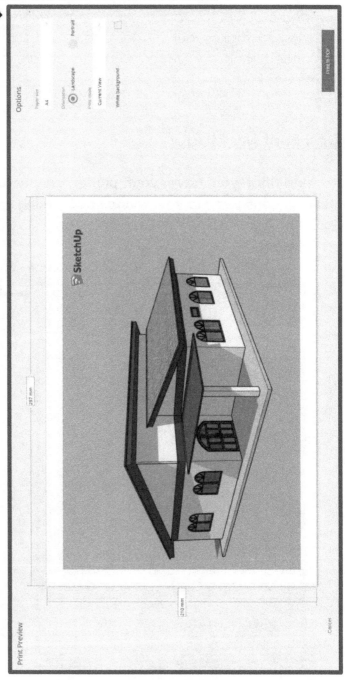

- The Preview indicates the current size of paper and In the **top right corner,** you have the **Options - Paper size, Orientation etc.**
- In the **bottom right corner - Print to PDF.**

- **Pick - Print to PDF**
- **The message**

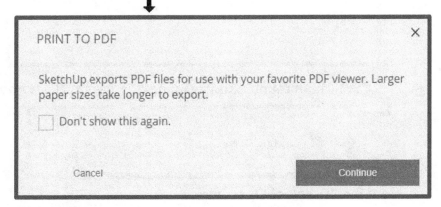

Is shown.

- **Pick** the **Continue button.**
- The message - **PREPARING TO PRINT...** is displayed, along with the progress slider.

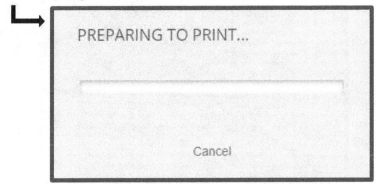

(The print preparation may take anywhere from a few seconds to a few minutes to complete).

- On completion, the SketchUp Graphics Screen is displayed, **showing your model,** and in the **bottom left corner,** below the undo/redo arrows, **you have the name of the model. -**

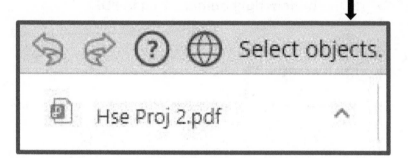

- **Pick the hidden menu arrowhead** next to the model name.

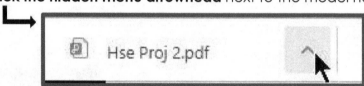

- **From the list, select Open.**

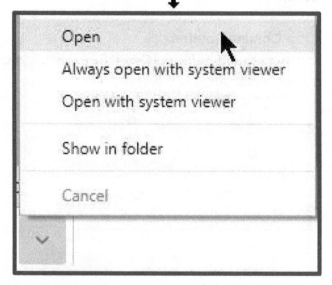

- The **Print Window** is displayed showing **Printer information, and a print preview of the model.**

The Basics - Part Two

The Print Window

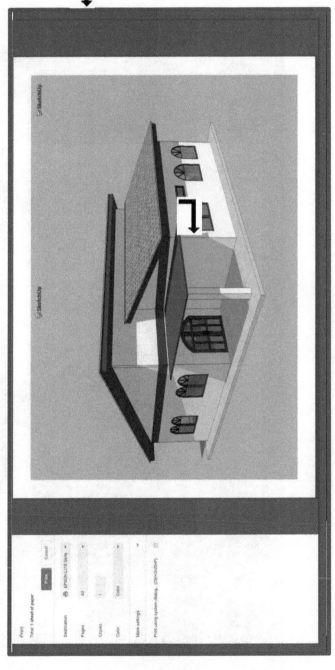

- **Pick the Print button**
  - A screen view of the model being printed is displayed.

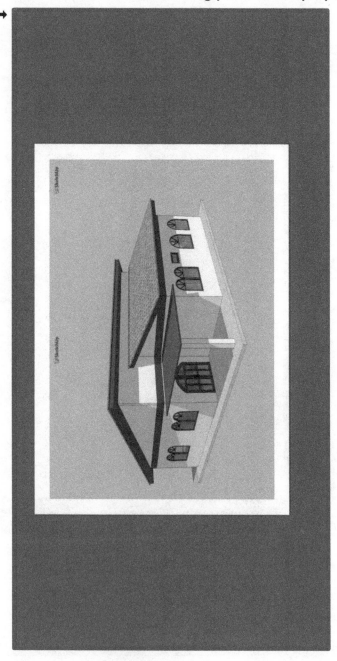

The Basics - Part Two

- Your printer starts to print your model.

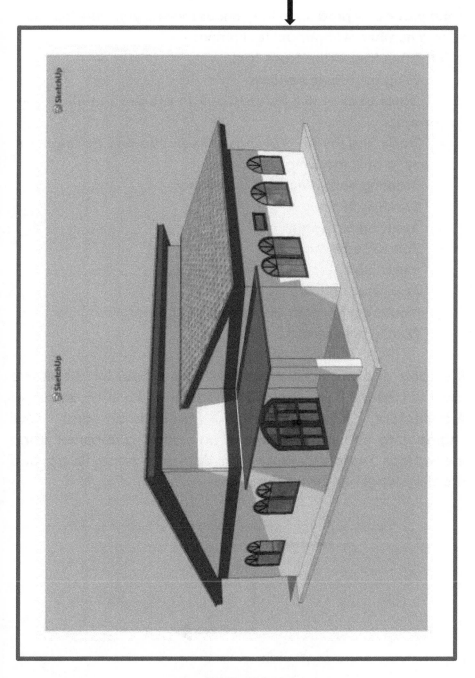

Summary

In the process of producing the various models you were introduced to a number of important techniques:-
- Other uses of the Erase Tool.
- Using Face Style options.
- Other uses of the Move/Copy to produce multi-copies (arrays).
- Producing layout drawings in SketchUp and getting them ready to be turned into 3D Models.
- Creating Walls, Windows and Doors.
- Creating Roofs.
- Applying Materials.
- How to Scale Materials.
- Importing objects from the Warehouse.
- Applying Shadows.
- Producing a simple Sky and Ground cover.
- Printing your model

The Tools and methods employed throughout this book are used constantly in the 3D modelling in the areas of Architecture, Interior Design, Mechanical and Civil Engineering, Set Design, and many other disciplines using the various SketchUp Programs. You now need to go and practice what has been shown.

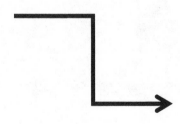

DETAILED CONTENTS OF PART ONE

The Basics - Part Two

The Basics - Part Two

The Basics - Part Two

The Basics - Part Two

The Basics - Part Two

The Basics - Part Two

The Basics - Part Two

DETAILED CONTENTS OF PART TWO

The Basics - Part Two

The Basics - Part Two

The Basics - Part Two

ARCHITECTURAL MODELLING

The Basics - Part Two

The Basics - Part Two

The Basics - Part Two

The Basics - Part Two